SPARKS
IN THE
DARK

Other Books by the Author
Holding On to Heaven With Hell on Your Back

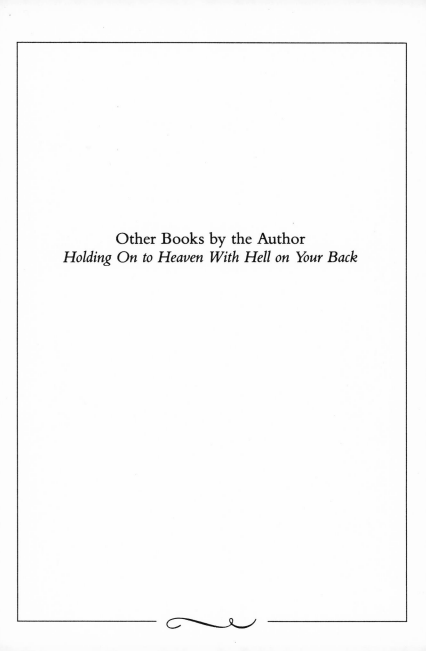

SPARKS IN THE DARK

Sheila Walsh Miller

A JANET THOMA BOOK

THOMAS NELSON PUBLISHERS
Nashville

Published in Nashville, Tennessee, by Thomas Nelson, Inc., and
distributed in Canada by Lawson Falle, Ltd., Cambridge,
Ontario.
Scripture quotations are from the NEW KING JAMES
VERSION of the Bible. Copyright © 1979, 1980, 1982, Thomas
Nelson, Inc., Publishers.

Library of Congress Cataloging-in-Publication Data

Miller, Sheila Walsh, 1956–
    Sparks in the dark / Sheila Walsh Miller.
      p.   cm.
    ISBN 0-8407-7769-8
    1. Christian life—1960–   2. Miller, Sheila Walsh, 1956–
I. Title.
BV4501.2.M495   1992
242—dc20   92–13104
                                              CIP

Printed in the United States of America
1 2 3 4 5 6 7 - 97 96 95 94 93 92

CONTENTS

INTRODUCTION

I remember as a young girl at summer camp being enthralled by bonfires. The flames danced in circles before my eyes, painting pictures that vanished before I took them in. Tiny sparks flew off in a bid for freedom. For a moment I believed they would start a new flame, but then they would be snuffed out by the chilled night air. One spark lived a brighter life one evening. It landed in a pile of leaves, and before we realized what was happening, this tiny light had become its own fire.

Sparks are like that. Some illumine the darkness for a moment and then they are gone. Some sparks land at the right moment, in the right place, and change things forever.

In the last few years, I have begun to understand that I will not be the same person tomorrow that I am today. Every day I am faced with choices and the way I respond will imprint my heart forever. I found it easy to quote "all things work together for good to those who love

God and are called according to His purpose" until I met a woman who had lost her husband and two children. I was confident in "He will give His angels charge over thee, lest you dash your foot against a stone" until I met a state trooper with burns over 40 percent of his body. I sang, "We are one in the spirit, we one in the Lord" with conviction until I came face to face with racism in the church.

Some will say that my questions and my willingness to acknowledge pain have caused me to have less faith today than I did yesterday. But I cannot live with my head in the sand. If we truly have a gospel for the world, it will withstand our tears, our questions, and our search for reality.

In these pages you will read the stories of fellow pilgrims. Through their diverse backgrounds, denominations, and nationalities, I see a common thread: Each one has appeared as a spark to me. Some lit up the darkness for a triumphant moment and then disappeared, while others lit a fire that still burns today. None of us would choose the path of suffering; none of us enjoy believing when we can't see our prayers being answered. None of us like seeing the darker side of ourselves and having to change. Yet, I have watched these pilgrims who have walked these paths, and there is no denying that they know something more. We all say, "God's strength is made perfect in our weakness," but they know it. We say, "I can do all things through Christ who strengthens me," but they know it. We sing, "Even though I walk through the valley of the shadow of death, even there thy rod and thy staff shall comfort me," but these believers have leaned upon that staff and been held up.

A friend once suggested that all churches in America be closed down. "Who needs them?" he said bitterly. The truth is, we all do. From Wall Street to the poorest barrio slums of L.A., from the northern mountains to the deep South, "People need the Lord." Our hearts cry for truth. We can pretend in a singles' bar. The church must be a place where we tell the truth about ourselves and embrace each other in all our human frailty, knowing that the value God places on human life is the life of his own Son, Jesus.

We have been commissioned, "You are the light of the world" (Matt. 5:14). I pray that some of these stories will make you smile and some will mist your eyes, but most of all, I pray that God will begin to send sparks into your darkness and fan the flames with His Holy Spirit so you can be a light to the world.

SPARKS IN THE DARK

More Than Conquerors

Yet in all these things we are more than conquerors through Him who loved us.
Romans 8:37

I was watching "The Honeymooners" at home when our telephone rang. Norman gave me a "here-we-go-again" look as I went to answer it. I had innocently put our name and number in the telephone directory, and now we were being bombarded by calls from 700 Club viewers.

"I'm sorry for calling you at home like this," a young woman's voice apologized on the other end of the line. From the other room, I could hear Ralph Kramden telling Alice she was the greatest. The show was over.

"That's all right," I replied. "How can I help you?"

Her name was Debbie. You may remember her story from my book, *Holding On to Heaven with Hell on Your Back.* Debbie has multiple sclerosis and bone cancer. She is in constant pain and seldom sleeps.

Debbie's call that night was the beginning of a friendship that has deeply touched and transformed my life in the last two years.

"No one will talk to me about death," Debbie told me that first night we talked on the phone. "No one will help me die as a believer."

I was so intrigued by her honesty I invited her to visit me for a weekend. Before she came, I prepared myself mentally to see a sick young woman. But when she arrived at my home in Virginia Beach and we met face-to-face, I was shocked.

Debbie was in her late twenties then and weighed about eighty pounds. Her cheeks were sunken. But there was a spark of life and humor in her eyes.

I hugged her gingerly, afraid she might crumble under a warm embrace, and greeted her mother, who had come with her on the trip. The three of us sat down in my living room. As we talked, I became aware of how much Debbie loves Jesus. She knows (and I know) God can heal her, but it doesn't look as if He will—her death seems imminent. Debbie shared how many have sat by her bed and, like Job's comforters, told her there must be some secret sin in her life. (I wonder if they feel her lack of healing reflects badly on their prayer lives.) This "comfort" has left her to bear her pain alone. But in the midst of this spiritual maelstrom, Debbie still trusts Jesus.

I, on the other hand, have struggled with Debbie's pain. I can accept her inevitable death. I believe that "to be absent from the body [is] to be present with the Lord" (2 Cor. 5:8), so death is something we can all look forward to. We are waiting for death to bring us face to

face with God. But I struggle to accept the suffering Debbie must endure before her death.

Debbie called me one night over a year after we had met. The pain was more than she could bear, and she needed to talk.

After a long conversation, I hung up the phone, angry with God. "If You're not going to heal her," I cried out, "then take her home. Why, why must she suffer so much now?"

I opened my Bible and read in Romans 8:

"For Your sake we are killed all day long;
    We are accounted as sheep for the slaughter."
Yet in all these things we are more than
    conquerors through Him who loved us.

Debbie isn't being a conqueror, I thought. *It seems as if she is being conquered daily.*

I stayed up all night struggling to make sense of this horror. I would love to tell you I found the answer to my question about why Debbie must suffer. But I didn't. I did find, however, a key to being conquerors: faith and the love of God.

Paul wrote to the Romans about the sufferings he and his companions endured. Their flesh was tormented, sometimes daily, but they were conquerors because they believed in God and trusted His love through Christ. "Neither death nor life, nor angels nor principalities nor powers, nor things present nor things to come, nor height nor depth, nor any other created thing, shall be able to separate us from the love of God which is in

Christ Jesus our Lord" (Rom. 8:38–39). Knowing nothing would keep God from loving them, Paul and his companions were able to keep believing in God and loving Him by walking with Him and proclaiming the gospel.

Conquerors are satisfied to know God loves them. Pain and death may destroy their bodies. But they know their souls will live forever because of the love of God. Thus, conquerors can live with unanswered questions. They don't confine God to a box of neatly packaged answers. They are able to depend on God without demanding explanations as if God "owed" them something.

Shadrach, Meshach, and Abed-Nego faced death with faith and love for God. King Nebuchadnezzar had ordered all of his subjects to worship false gods. When Shadrach, Meshach, and Abed-Nego refused, Nebuchadnezzar commanded that they be thrown into a furnace for their disloyalty. "God will save us," they told Nebuchadnezzar, "but even if He doesn't, we still refuse to worship your idols." Even if God did not save their bodies from the fire, these three men believed in God's greatness and power and love. They loved God in return through their obedience to Him, by continuing to worship him and by not bowing down to the idols of the king.

Although she has not been healed, pain and death have not destroyed God's love for Debbie nor has Debbie's love for Jesus been destroyed. Debbie believes in God's love, so she can remain faithful until she is with God in heaven.

Our comfort is knowing God is for us and nothing can keep us from His love. Our God is not impotent. His love overcomes the powers of life and death and makes us more than conquerors.

Sometimes Dreams Come True

> Then the LORD answered me and said:
> "Write the vision
> And make it plain on tablets,
> That he may run who reads it.
> For the vision is yet for an appointed time;
> But at the end it will speak,
> and it will not lie.
> Though it tarries, wait for it;
> Because it will surely come,
> It will not tarry."
> Habakkuk 2:2–3

*D*ecember 19, 1982, stands out for Pat and Jill Williams as their "darkest hour." They were the epitome of the happily married Christian couple. Pat had been the general manager of the Philadelphia 76'ers for twelve years and the Chicago Bulls for four, and was now working with the team Orlando Magic. Basketball was his life and he was surrounded by the material things that success provides.

But despite Pat's success, Jill was unhappy. For years Jill had felt neglected, but never voiced her frustrations.

Deep down she felt as if Pat had never cared for her and always had better things to do with his time. And on that December day, Jill exploded. She told Pat that she hated her marriage and didn't think she still loved him.

Pat was devastated. He had no idea his wife was so miserable and didn't know what to do. He remembered being told once that "for God to do an impossible work, He must take an impossible man and crush him." And he believed he was this impossible man.

Pat cried out to God for help, and God began to show him that he had been on a success trip—everything in his life was self-motivated and self-gratifying. From that point on Pat made his marriage his number-one priority.

Jill had had a childhood dream of adopting Asian children, which Pat had dismissed as a childish unrealistic fantasy, but he began to think again. Three days before Christmas, he was standing in line at a turkey farm, waiting to pick up a fresh turkey, when he saw a little Asian face smiling up at him over the shoulder of the man in front of him. Pat saw that the parents were a Caucasian couple and asked them about their little one. They had adopted the baby from Korea through Holt International Children's Services.

Pat rushed home to tell Jill about this new possibility. Initially she was resistant, struggling to believe her dreams could be coming true, but in a few days, she was convinced. By the following September, they were enjoying a renewed marriage and were the proud parents of two Korean sisters—Andrea, aged two, and Sarah, aged three—who had been abandoned on the doorstep of a Seoul police station.

In the following years, Jill gave birth to four children, so now there were six children.

The family moved from Philadelphia when Pat signed a contract to become the president and general manager of the Orlando Magic N.B.A. team. They were enjoying a full and hectic life, yet they felt in their hearts that they had room for more children. Jill heard about six-year-old Korean twin boys who had no one to take care of them. The idea of adopting twins intrigued the whole family. So on May 1, 1987, they welcomed Thomas and Stephen into their home. And now there were eight!

Meanwhile, on the other side of the world in the Philippine Islands, four little brothers had been abandoned by their mother. They managed to survive on the streets for two years without starving to death until they landed on the doorstep of a Christian orphanage and were taken in.

One day a copy of *Moody Monthly* arrived for Louise, who ran the home. She read the magazine and then left it out on a table for anyone else to browse through. On the front cover were Pat and Jill Williams and eight happy faces. The boys picked up the magazine and studied those expressions, then went to Louise's office and knocked on her door. "Can we go and live with the Williams family?" they asked.

From the chair where she was sitting, Louise looked into the boys' expectant faces and wondered how she could tell them that it simply wasn't possible. The telephone on her desk rang. "Hello—excuse me?"

The Holt Agency was calling from America. Pat and

Jill Williams had just seen a picture of the four boys and wanted to adopt them.

In November 1988, four little boys stepped off a plane at the Orlando International Airport and into the arms of the Williams family. Then there were twelve!

I laughed and cried with Pat and Jill as they told their story, and thoughts flooded my mind. If Jill hadn't given her marriage a second chance, where would she be today? Perhaps she would be alone and isolated. And where would all these little ones be? I imagine they would have found homes, but none more loving and joy filled and noisy than Pat and Jill's.

Sometimes it seems as if our hopes and dreams have died, but, if they truly are of God, they will not be late in becoming real—not one single day. God can make the impossible possible if we will hold on to Him in the dark times. It would be sad to give up just one day before our miracle happens. If we only lean on what we see, we will often despair, but God has promised that when the time is right, dreams really do come true.

> Teach me Lord to wait on you
> for I would run ahead
> Teach me Lord to rest in you
> And calm this fearful dread
> Teach me Lord that you are true
> your words will never fail
> and I will live to see
> each promise that you give fulfilled.

A Voice from the Grave

And Jesus said to him, "Assuredly, I say to you,
today you will be with Me in Paradise."
Luke 23:43

*M*ost of the film people I interview are on-camera
personalities. I rarely have the opportunity to talk with
"the brains behind the scenes," like Bryan Hickox. Before I ever met Bryan, I was familiar with his work as a
director. I had enjoyed "Troop Beverly Hills," with Shel-
ley Long, and was impressed by "Small Sacrifices,"
which starred Farrah Fawcett.

As a Christian in Hollywood, Bryan desires to illumi-
nate life. He looks for stories that uphold integrity and
morality, without forcing religious ideology. His is a
strong voice for truth and humanity in a bent and dehu-
manizing world.

Bryan appeared on my show one day to discuss a CBS
after-school special called "Dead Wrong." Usually, I
view movie clips before we go on the air, but that day the

clips were being edited up until air time. So I was unprepared for what I was about to see.

"Dead Wrong" told the story of John Evans III, who was imprisoned and sentenced to death by electrocution for killing a pawnbroker in front of his young family. It was a brutal and heartless crime.

While in prison, John came face to face with Jesus Christ, and he cried out to Jesus to save his soul. His conversion was like that of the thief on the cross who asked Jesus to show mercy on him in his last moments on earth. As Jesus was hanging on the cross, the criminal on one side of Him joined the mocking crowds: "If You are the Christ, save Yourself and us." But the thief on the other side recognized Jesus and responded to the criminal, "Do you not even fear God, seeing you are under the same condemnation? And we indeed justly, for we receive the due reward of our deeds; but this Man has done nothing wrong" (Luke 23:40–41). The thief recognized his need and his Savior. And he received the promise of being with Jesus in paradise that very day.

John Evans' glorious conversion came in the last days before his death. Knowing that he had little time left to serve the Lord, he made a strange and courageous choice. He asked to have his last day, including his execution, filmed as a warning to others.

Tears rolled down my cheeks as I watched John Evans' mother come to say good-bye. A devout woman, she had prayed for John for many years. Now that her prayers had been answered, she was being called on to say good-bye to him. She clung to her son until the prison

guards told her that she had to leave. "I'll be seeing you, Mom," John cried after her. Then they took John Evans III and strapped him to the electric chair and took a life for a life.

This is the only time I've been unable to finish a program. As the director and cameramen waited for me to close the show, I sat and wept. I wept for his mother. I wept for a wasted life. I wept because he never knew God's love till the last moments. Most of all, I wept with joy knowing that the gates of the Kingdom of Heaven had opened that day and God had welcomed this repentant man home. That day John Evans was with Jesus in paradise.

God's mercy is limitless. We don't have to wait until a near-death experience to receive His grace. But God will never turn us away when we come to Him in repentance. Seeing the mercy of our God in the life of John Evans, I wrote the lyrics for "The Third Cross."

The Third Cross

A wasted life now it's too late
No time to make amends
No time to put things straight
As Madness called him to the edge
He looked down through the years
Held for all to see upon the third cross.

In blinding pain he fought for breath
Wondered when this hell began
Wondered when this hell would end
The anguish in his mother's eyes
Tore his heart in two
As she watched her baby stretched
Upon the third cross.

Upon the third cross a dying man
Upon the third cross his life is gone
Upon the third cross his guilt is shown
And justice will be served on the third cross.

An angry crowd, he heard them cry,
"Save yourself, Son of God
Save yourself or die,"
He heard the man beside him say
"Forgive them Father please,"
As they tore his clothes in two
Beneath the third cross.

His hour had come, he felt it near
"God, if there is any mercy,

God, I beg you, can you hear?"
And as he turned his head
He looked upon the Lamb of God
And Love was shining down upon
The third cross.

For in that moment time stood still
And fear and death were gone
As he cried, "Lord Jesus, remember
Me, when you come into your own."

Upon the third cross
A dying man
Upon the third cross
His guilt is shown
But mercy flowed that day
On the third cross.

Fragile Magnolias

You will keep him in perfect peace,
Whose mind is stayed on You.
Isaiah 26:3

*S*ome of the most powerfully moving films are those that stir memories in our hearts. I went to see "Steel Magnolias" because I like Sally Field and Olympia Dukakis, but I sat weeping in the theater at the end because of the memories it stirred of a woman I'd known. The members of our church had watched and prayed and begged God for the life of this vibrant young wife and mother. Then we stood beside her heartbroken parents and husband and little boy and buried her.

I didn't realize when I watched "Steel Magnolias" that it was based on a true story. But two months after I'd seen it, I met the real husband. His name is Pat Robinson and his wife's name was Susan, not Shelby. Pat is a pediatrician, who, as a nine-year-old boy, was scared into the kingdom of God by a hellfire and brimstone message he believed into adulthood.

Pat and Susan married, knowing she had a severe form

of diabetes that made it risky for her to have a baby. But Susan longed for a child, so when she conceived, she was overjoyed.

Some time after the birth of their baby, Susan became sick. Pat decided this was a test from God and he was not going to fail. He believed God was going to dramatically heal his wife as a testimony to all around her.

But Susan was not healed; in fact, she became worse. Weakened and discouraged by her sickness, she felt as if she were a failure. She believed that she had not been healed because she had no faith. So Pat decided that it would be up to him—he could save his wife.

The day Susan died, Pat was in disbelief. He stood beside her bed, and the doctors told him she was gone. But he couldn't take it in. How had he failed? How could he have been so wrong?

Pat left Susan's room and paced the halls of the hospital, wringing his hands and rubbing his forehead. He thought until it all became clear to him—God was going to wait until the funeral and raise Susan out of the casket! Excitement surged through him as he realized how much more impressive this miracle would be than had Susan been healed. He could barely contain himself and found it hard not to tell anyone what was going to happen.

He sat through Susan's memorial service on the edge of his pew. All around him, family members wept, but he watched the casket and waited. Susan didn't sit up. The pall bearers lowered her coffin into the ground. The lid remained closed as the men threw earth over the top of it.

Pat's life crumpled like the sod on the casket. The well-meaning friends who had told him, "If you have enough faith, Susan will be healed" disappeared like the morning mist, and he was left alone with a God he didn't know.

Depression blanketed his heart in the following days, as he stared into a bleak and empty future. In his loneliness, he began to cry out to God. Every day he would open his Bible and read of a God who promised peace in the midst of turmoil and joy in the deepest sorrow. At first, Pat's hopelessness made him feel as if he were losing his mind, and he asked God to hold on to him. As he kept his mind on God's Word and the promises that he read there, peace began to edge out his despair. He read, "You will keep him in perfect peace, / Whose mind is stayed on You." He asked God to strip him of the lies and half truths the enemy loves to whisper in our ears, and reduce him to simple truth.

"Perfect peace" is translated from the Hebrew *shalom shalom,* which signifies fulfillment, abundance, well-being, security. The phrase "Whose mind is stayed on You" comes from two Hebrew words: the first meaning "will, imagination"; the second, "dependent, supported, firm." When our wills and imaginations are dependent on God, when we choose to turn our thoughts to God, we can find the simple truth that God is enough. We find out, as Isaiah wrote, that "in the LORD, is everlasting strength." And in His strength, we discover fulfillment and security.

Our faith in God is not enough to bring about mira-

cles. God takes home some faithful servants before we are ready to say good-bye. And He allows people with no faith at all to be healed. All we can do in the time of grief is set our minds on Him—believe God is enough, even if the miracles don't come—for He alone can hold us through the night.

Walk in Truth

Teach me Your way, O LORD;
I will walk in Your truth;
Unite my heart to fear Your name.
Psalm 86:11

I've struggled with telling the truth since I was a little girl. I remember one day when I was about ten years old, my Mom was expecting guests for dinner. She spent hours getting everything ready. Fifteen minutes before her guests were to arrive, I went upstairs to my room to see if I could find something to play with. I was bored.

The previous Christmas, an aunt had given me a glass dog filled with bubble bath and I decided that this would be a good thing to play with now. I sat on the top stair and gave it a little push to see if it could bounce off every step on its way down. Halfway down it had gathered so much momentum that it broke and the contents spilled all over the stair carpet.

My mom called from the kitchen and asked what I

was doing. I told her that I had dropped my piggy bank and everything was fine.

I tried to mop up the soap by rubbing it, but it foamed and foamed, until I was up to my neck in white froth. I will never forget the horrified look on my mother's face as she came into the hallway to answer the doorbell and saw me sitting on the stairs like a rabid dog, foaming at the mouth.

As I lay in bed that night, with a rather warm posterior, my mother's words rang in my ears. "I'm not punishing you because you dropped your dog; I'm punishing you because you lied to me."

What makes us afraid of telling the truth? Perhaps we fear rejection once the truth about us is known. Perhaps we wonder if people would love and accept us if they saw us as we are.

At times, I've caught myself telling a story or recounting what happened at a concert or conference differently from how it was. Five hundred people may have attended a conference, but in my story eight hundred showed. Ten people may have been saved at a concert, but in my story, fifteen were saved. It's ridiculous to exaggerate what God has done. Deep down, I must feel that results impress people rather than character. But I don't think I'm alone in this.

I agreed to sing at a crusade for a lesser known evangelist, whom I had met at a conference. This man impressed me with his sincerity and his heart for evangelism, so I was happy to participate in the event.

The evening of the crusade was a good one. About a

thousand people attended, and at the end of the message, about fifty people came forward.

A few months later, this gentleman's newsletter came to me in the mail. I flipped past exciting stories of recent crusades to the article about the conference I had participated in. According to the article, about five thousand people had attended the conference, and more than a thousand responded to the gospel message. I was horrified.

As I sat in my office, full of "righteous indignation," I felt the Lord holding a mirror in front of my face, and I looked strangely like my exaggerating friend.

David's prayer in Psalm 86 has become a source of encouragement for me since this experience. "Teach me Your way, O LORD; / I will walk in Your truth." David wanted to live according to God's will and according to the truth about God. He also wanted a "united heart"—a heart that stayed focused on the truth about God, a heart that was not wandering from the truth—so he could fear, honor, God.

The truth is God is great; He is full of power and mercy and care. David had recognized this truth and was praising God for it: "For You, Lord, are good, and ready to forgive. . . . For You are great, and do wondrous things." When we trust God's greatness and mercy as David did, we are free of the need to affirm our own names and can instead "fear [God's] name."

I keep myself on a tight reign now, and if I blow it, I publicly apologize and correct myself. God is truth and anything else, no matter how mild-mannered, comes

from the father of all lies. I pray I will fear the Lord more than I fear my fellow man. I don't want to give the enemy a foothold in my life; I want to walk in the light. I've decided to stop exaggerating even if it takes me sixteen million years to get there!

Celibate, Yes. Dead, No.

I charge you, O daughters of Jerusalem,
Do not stir up nor awaken love
Until it pleases.
Song of Solomon 8:4

*S*exuality and the single Christian—we don't talk about it, but *thousands* of single Christians are sexually active. While in the general marketplace, sexuality is freely and openly discussed, it's still a fairly taboo subject in religious environments. Do we think sex will go away if we don't mention the word?

AIDS and the prevalence of other sexually transmitted diseases are increasing the popularity of sexual abstinence, but the roots of abstinence are fear rather than conviction.

In most congregations, virtue is assumed but not taught. When I first got on a horse, I assumed I could ride it. I fell off. We can't assume everyone entering the doors of the church shares the same convictions about purity. We need to talk about it.

Julia Duin, a writer for the *Houston Chronicle,* speaks

out passionately and honestly about Christian purity. She feels that many women sense time slipping away and agree to premarital sex out of a desire to bond with a man, hoping marriage will come later. Couples sometimes do feel obligated to marry out of a sense of guilt, conviction, or duty after they have been sexually active. I have known many of these marriages to fall apart because one or both spouses ended up feeling tricked or used.

As we approach our thirties, the sands of time seem to be falling ever quicker through our fingertips. Singles experience pressure in the workplace to make their careers their lives. The young and upwardly mobile are a hot commodity because of their energy and motivation. Corporations capitalize on this by demanding more of them, leaving them little time to develop relationships outside of work and feeling alone and abandoned.

We tend to turn to what will give us immediate relief from pain, rather than choose what will satisfy us for the long term. With limited time and resources (open late every night of the week, bars are the most available resource for relationships), singles are even more prone to look in every crowded room for love rather than find people who will remind them of God's loving presence in their lives.

The Song of Solomon describes a passionate romance between a man and a woman, "the Shulamite." They long for one another; they search the streets for one another when they are apart. At the end of the book, the Shulamite says that this love had made her "as one who

found peace." The couple experiences ecstasy and peace through their relationship. Yet, throughout the book, we hear this refrain from the woman:

> I charge you, O daughters of Jerusalem, . . .
> Do not stir up nor awaken love
> Until it pleases.

The Shulamite tells her friends not to stimulate love falsely. Don't arouse love before its time, she warns them. The joy of the relationship she has found makes the wait worth it. She can receive this love as a gift because she has not demanded it or taken it for herself, which multiplies her enjoyment of the passion.

It is difficult to wait for what we so desperately want to experience in our lives. But as we trust God's love for us and constantly choose the better way—obedience to Him—we will ultimately experience a peace and a joy we would not trade for anything the world can offer.

I was celibate until I married at twenty-five. Big deal, you may say. But for me it was a big deal. I was thankful I had said no to the constant temptation I faced before then.

The first couple of times we say no are the hardest. But as we continue to be faithful to Christ, our strength will increase and we will not give away our virginity on a whim. When faced with temptation, cry out to God. He is not easily shocked. He welcomes your honesty and understands your desires. He will uphold you when you are holding on by your fingertips. "God can't hold my

hand," I heard a friend say. No, but as I wrote in my lyric at the end of this story, He can hold your heart until it's time to give it away.

Paul wrote to the Ephesians to speak "to one another psalms and hymns and spiritual songs, singing and making melody in your heart to the Lord, giving thanks always for all things to God the Father in the name of our Lord Jesus Christ, submitting to one another in the fear of God" (Eph. 5:19–21). Paul stressed the importance of believers' encouraging each other with Scripture. We need the freedom to be honest with each other about our sexual desires and feelings of loneliness, but after we've been honest, we need to encourage each other with Scriptures about God's love for us and His desire to be intimate with us.

We also need people who will remind us of the charges in Scripture to remain pure, such as Paul's charge to Timothy: "Let no one despise your youth, but be an example to the believers in word, in conduct, in love, in spirit, in faith, in purity" (1 Tim. 4:12). Without these relationships, we will forget that God longs for intimacy with us, and we will begin to search the world and every crowded room for love.

> I stand here on this moonlit night
> And long to share this moment
> With someone who'd die for me.
> I walk along a lonely beach and cry out
> To the wind to bring my love to me.
> So maker of the stars and sand

The one who walks with wounded
    hands
Please hold me now
And in your arms I'll lay my head
And rest my dreams
Until you call them from the dead.

For the Little Ones

> "Let your light so shine before men, that they may see your good works and glorify your Father in heaven."
> Matthew 5:16

One of the hottest issues debated in our nation is abortion. In the fall of 1991, the stage for this debate was the Congressional hearings that determined Judge Clarence Thomas's suitability for Supreme Court Justice. I watched as Congress questioned Judge Clarence Thomas. With sickening predictability, Judge Thomas was repeatedly asked his position on abortion.

What kind of a nation do we live in, I wondered, *where one of the key issues that determines a judge's suitability for confirmation is his or her willingness to allow a woman to take the life of her unborn child? Has the world gone mad while we were all sleeping?*

Each of us must decide where we stand on this issue and by prayer or protest let our voices be heard. But what happens when the issue leaves the playground and comes knocking at our door? What choices will we

make? And how will we respond to the choices of the individuals we meet in our homes and at our churches?

Not long after Norman and I were married, I thought I was pregnant. I paced the one-bedroom apartment where we were living, horrified at this unforeseen turn of events. I looked around me and saw no room for little feet. Financially, things were tight. A large business venture Norman was involved with had just fallen apart and I could tell from the lines across his forehead that he was truly concerned. I could hear myself saying to him, "Hey Norman, you know how we're really in a mess financially? Well, guess what? I'm pregnant."

My fears mounting, I tried to escape to the shopping mall, where I walked around aimlessly, protected from other shoppers by a wall of incredulity. I sat down with a cup of coffee, wondering if coffee was harmful to a baby, and reviewed my options. How could I tell Norman I was pregnant knowing how worried he already was about our future?

A silver strand of hope suddenly lighted on my shoulder. *I don't have to have this baby,* I thought. *I have a choice.* I couldn't believe how appealing those words were and quickly dispelled them, walking out into the crisp clean air.

I later discovered that I wasn't pregnant. But I remained in disbelief that I had entertained the thought of having an abortion. In the midst of despair, most of us reach for a quick fix. But abortion does not provide a quick fix for anyone.

A young woman wept bitterly for an hour after a concert of mine one evening, as she talked of her experience.

She had chosen to get rid of her baby so she could pursue her career. The procedure had been quick and relatively painless, and as she walked out into the sun afterward, she felt her troubles were over. But as the weeks turned into months, she found it hard to sleep. She burst into tears for no apparent reason. And when she would see a child walking beside its mother, she would wonder, *What would my baby have looked like?* As she sat with her head in her hands that evening, she asked me, "Why didn't they tell me I would feel this way?"

Abortion has been carefully and neatly packaged in this country. Our consciences have been anesthetized to make the unthinkable reasonable. But after the act, the anesthetic wears off, leaving countless women wondering how they could have done such a thing. I have friends who have had abortions, and I know that forgiveness and comfort can be found at Jesus' feet. For those of you with fragmented souls, I urge you to fall into the healing arms of Jesus.

In a discussion about the Jewish holocaust, I heard a man ask, "Where were all the Christians in Germany when six million Jews were being slaughtered?" I had asked that question before; yet as I listened that day, the abortion issue pressed on my mind. *How could we all be so blind?* I wondered. It's easy to see the sin and shame that rests at other people's doors and not see the blood on our own hands.

There will come a day when we will answer not only for what we have done, but for what we have failed to do. Jesus told His disciples in His Sermon on the Mount that they were the "light of the world." People don't buy

lamps and hide them under a bushel, Jesus said. Instead, they set them on a stand and let them "[give] light to all who are in the house." Similarly, the disciples were not to hide but to "shine before men, that they may see your good works." Jesus wanted His disciples to let the world know they were His children by their works. Then, men would "glorify your Father in heaven" (Matt. 5:13–16).

God will be glorified not only when we are faithful to live according to the truth—to withstand the temptation of seeking a "quick fix"—but when we help others to see His truth.

Phil Keaggy wrote of the urgency of speaking the truth on behalf of the unborn children in his song "Little Ones":

> Who will speak up for the little ones
> Helpless and half abandoned.
> They've got a right to choose life;
> They don't want to lose.
> I've got to speak up, won't you?*

From Christ to the Church

> Praying always . . . and for me, that utterance may
> be given to me, that I may open my mouth boldly
> to make known the mystery of the gospel.
> Ephesians 6:18–19

I saw a woman at a Christian conference, wearing a T-shirt that said, "Pray for me. I'm a pastor's wife." I caught her eye and we smiled, but something behind her smile disturbed me and made me think, *It must be pretty hard to lead a congregation of people, particularly Christians.*

We are all so different, with varied opinions on how everything should be done and little reluctance in sharing those opinions. I know that from some of the letters I receive at the Christian Broadcasting Network. I have been called everything from an angel in disguise to a Jezebel out to pull unsuspecting men into my clutches. (Believe me, most of the time I am way too tired to clutch at anyone or anything apart from Norman, my dog, Charlie, and a Big Mac!)

I don't remember much about the theme of the conference, but I did gain a fresh desire to pray for pastors

and their families. I know how easy it is to become so busy doing things for God that you lose friendship with Him. There have been many days when I have felt discouraged and alone in my Christian walk and have asked the Lord to tell me what I have done to break fellowship with Him. Sometimes all I've needed is a good night's rest and a kind word.

Paul had every opportunity to feel this way too. He was beaten and imprisoned for preaching the gospel. Yet, he never lost heart. In the book of Acts, we read that Paul prayed and sang hymns while he was in prison. Paul wrote his epistle to the Philippians from prison. The theme of the letter was the need to have joy in all circumstances.

Prayer played an important part in giving Paul the endurance he had. Paul opened more than one of his letters, acknowledging his prayers for believers. And in more than one of his letters, he asked believers to pray for him. To the Ephesians he said, "[Pray] for me, . . . that I may open my mouth boldly to make known the mystery of the gospel." Pray "that God would open to us a door for the word, to speak the mystery of Christ, for which I am also in chains," Paul said in Colossians. "Brethren, pray for us," he wrote the Thessalonians. "[P]ray for us, that the word of the Lord may have free course and be glorified." And to Philemon, he wrote, "prepare a guest room for me, for I trust that through your prayers I shall be granted to you." Paul knew that believers were praying for him, and he trusted Christ to answer those prayers, thus gaining strength and faith to persevere in his ministry.

Our pastors and leaders need to have the same assurance—that we are praying for them. So I urge us all to pray faithfully for them and to do whatever we can to encourage them. Pray that their lives would be blameless and holy, above reproach. Pray that God will give your pastor wisdom as he studies and ears to hear the inner voice of the Holy Spirit. Pray that God will use him as a bridge builder in your community between other pastors and leaders.

Pastors are human beings too, and Satan rejoices every time a faithful shepherd falls. Don't be afraid to say, "You're doing a great job. We love you. Can we help with anything?" Pray that whenever he opens his mouth he will fearlessly make known the mystery of the gospel with his words. Why not surprise his wife and send her flowers telling her that you love and appreciate her too? Who knows? Perhaps if we did we might see a few "Thank the Lord. I'm a pastor's wife" shirts!

Unfinished Business

Therefore, putting away lying, each one speak
truth with his neighbor, for we are members of
one another.
Ephesians 4:25

I lay awake last night thinking about it—unfinished
business, little nagging things I have been meaning to do
for a while but somehow never have gotten to. I don't
know why they all came together in my mind in one
evening, but I lay awake and itemized my thoughts: *I owe
so and so a phone call—I know she feels neglected. I never apologized to that realtor for the misunderstanding between us.*

I didn't think anything on my list was vital, so I'd left
everything undone. *My friend knows that I care about her,* I
thought. *I don't really have to call. The miscommunication was
really the realtor's fault.* Yet, a dissatisfied feeling still created a slight film over my heart.

I hate confrontation. I hate facing unpleasant situa-
tions, particularly when I have blown it. Like many
others, when problems hit at work or at church or with
friends, I find it easier to succumb to the subtle tempta-

tion to move on—start over on a clean sheet of paper. This is a horrible way to live—and a terrible waste of paper. Think how many clean sheets we'd need!

When people outside the church who criticize our so-called new life see us avoiding the truth in our relationships, their criticism is justified. Salvation is not merely a ticket to heaven; it's a whole new journey.

We are "new" people, Paul said in his letter to the Ephesians. We used to be "alienated" from the life of God—foreigners, isolated, in the dark. But when Christ came to earth, He reconciled us to Himself and to one another; in Paul's words, we are now "members of one another."

On this new journey, we can live as new people. We "put on the new man" and "walk in love, as Christ also loved us." Paul wrote that we needed to maintain the love and unity of all of our relationships—family, marriage, friendships, church acquaintances. And the way to do that was by "putting away lying" and speaking the truth in love. We admit when we are wrong; we treat others with respect and dignity; we put the needs of others before our own. When we love others and live humbly before them, we are able to do for them what Christ did for us: we build bridges and restore relationships. And we maintain unity and love.

I have been finding freedom and strength in facing life and the consequences of my actions. At times, this means I experience pain. But it also means I can live without being afraid of stepping on something I've pushed under the rug. I no longer have to live as if on the edge of a volcano, waiting for something to blow. In-

stead, I can live freely, at peace with myself and others.

We are alive because we have been kissed by the giver of all life. He gave us a model for living life when He finished His business on the cross and now He expects us to live that way. That is the way to live.

On the Edge of a Volcano

On the edge of a volcano
I have lived for many years,
But it seems the distant rumble's
Getting louder in my ears.

I have tried to walk away from
Broken pieces of my past,
But their edges cut my feet
Like shattered glass.

I have tried to push disturbing thoughts
Beyond the reach of man.
I have tried to burn my bridges,
But I've only burned my hand
Brushing things under the carpet
Hoping that they'll go away,
But I feel I'll lose my balance any day.

Queen for a Day; Love for a Lifetime

Love . . . bears all things, believes all things, hopes
all things, endures all things.
1 Corinthians 13:7

I was wandering around in the fresh spring air of Williamsburg, Virginia, when I saw a young couple emerge
under a cloud of rice from the door of an old church. The
bride gazed lovingly into the eyes of the Mel Gibson
look-alike beside her. Friends and family, sharing in their
celebration of love, surrounded them. The girl in white
hugged her father one last time before getting into the
ribbon-streamed, modern-day carriage. She seemed
anxious to go, but the bridegroom still stood on the
sidewalk, almost hesitant.

I had this ridiculous urge to run up to the car and say,
"Look, don't panic! When it all starts to fall apart you
can make things work if you put God first." I'm happy
to tell you, I restrained myself!

I wish we talked more in our churches and homes

39

about the reality of marriage. In *Cinderella,* the wedding is the last page of the book. For this couple—in this life—it was not the last page, but the first of their life together. The years to follow would be filled with laughter and tears, passionate moments, and angry words.

God has taught me a sobering lesson in my ten years of marriage. When I walked out into the Scottish sunshine (also known as rain!) in my white dress, I thought I had found the answer to my problems. No more feelings of insecurity and self-hatred, no more loneliness, no more restlessness. In truth, I have experienced some of my loneliest, most insecure days during these ten years.

Marriage turned the spotlight on Norman and me, and we suddenly saw each other as we really are. Before we married, I would sometimes look at myself in the mirror in a new dress and think, *I wonder if I look a little fat in this?* Now I'd ask Norman, and he would tell me!

The more I became aware of how little I loved and accepted my flawed, human existence, the more I blamed Norman. You see, I thought marriage was supposed to make me happy. Now I know that marriage is supposed to make me more like Jesus, and the more like Jesus Norman and I become, the happier we will be together. I thought I knew what I needed to make me happy. I would look at other men and think, *Now that's what I need Norman to be like.* But God has shown me that I don't have a clue what I need. The grass is always greener on the other side, but it's only when you get up really close that you can see it's artificial turf.

I finally committed to stand on the covenant I had made with Norman before God, because I knew it was

the right thing to do. I hoped we would find a way of living together peacefully under one roof, friends, if nothing more.

There were many moments in the following year when I thought, *Who are you trying to kid, Sheila? There is no way you can do this.* During the darkest days of my marriage, my mother told me that I loved Norman more than I realized and that if I would hold on, the best days of my life were yet to come. At the time, holding on seemed impossible. Flooded by despair and weak from crying, I would come to Jesus and throw myself on His mercy and ask Him to help me. Sometimes you have to choose God in the darkness, trusting Him for what will be there when the morning breaks.

My mother's words have become a reality in my life. I never imagined for a moment that Norman and I could be as happy as we are. I love him with all my heart. We still occasionally have rows—some days I still look fat in a dress—but the emptiness in both of our hearts is being filled by Jesus, and He will never disappoint us.

I've discovered that when you bring the ashes of your broken dreams to the foot of the cross and allow the wind of the Holy Spirit to blow over them, you find that you are holding a diamond in the dust and you didn't know it and you almost threw it away. Love bears all things, believes all things, hopes all things, endures all things. Love rejoices with the truth. Norman and I have chosen to love each other and we have endured. We will never be enough for each other, but Jesus is and that's a cause for celebration.

As I walked back to my car on that spring day in Wil-

liamsburg, I prayed for the young couple and thought, *Perhaps ten years from now I'll be walking down that street again and stop to watch a wedding party. Out of the corner of my eye I'll see a couple standing, watching, holding hands, ten years older and wiser, and I'll know that they made it too!*

The Cord of Unforgiveness

"For if you forgive men their trespasses, your heavenly Father will also forgive you. But if you do not forgive men their trespasses, neither will your Father forgive your trespasses."
Matthew 6:14–15

*F*orgiveness is a tough one! It's very hard for many of us to forgive those who have wronged us in some way. I have had little to forgive and yet I struggle too. I have a particularly hard time with injustice.

My earliest memory of this is still a vivid one. My mother had recently painted the banister in our home and had banned sliding down it. But it was so tempting! The banister was long enough so I could pick up speed as I slid down and then could be launched into space at the other end. I fought with the flesh and lost. I positioned myself at the top of the stairs with my new sandals on and slid down. As I looked back I realized with horror that the buckle of my sandals had scraped all the way down, leaving a trench in the new paint. At that moment my brother, Stephen, appeared and said he was

going to tell my mom. I begged him not to (Didn't I realize that she would probably notice it?). He told me that if I gave him my large bag of candy that I had been saving for a showing of Cinderella on T.V. that afternoon, he would remain closemouthed.

I looked at the candy; I looked at the long scratch all the way down the railing. It was a painful decision, but I traded my bag of candy for his silence.

Stephen sat on the bottom stair and ate every piece. Then he went and told my mom! I was devastated! (I also had a very sore sit upon.) I was overwhelmed by the injustice of the situation, especially when my mother told me that it was my own fault.

A few years later I was faced with a more serious situation. A friend of mine lied about me to my two closest friends, and I could not defend myself without betraying the trust of someone dear to me. I spent many sleepless nights and wept many bitter tears, feeling helpless and betrayed. But in the midst of it all, I was faced with Christ's command to forgive so that my heavenly Father would forgive me.

I read Jesus' words on forgiveness in the Sermon on the Mount one afternoon. Jesus had been teaching the disciples to pray simply and in secret—not like the hypocrites who prayed on the street corners, vainly repeating themselves. The model for prayer He gave them included forgiving others and asking for God's forgiveness.

> "Our Father in heaven, . . .
>   . . . forgive us our debts,
> As we forgive our debtors" (Matt. 6:9–12).

At the close of the prayer, Jesus emphasized these two lines, saying, "For if you forgive men their trespasses, your heavenly Father will also forgive you. But if you do not forgive men their trespasses, neither will your Father forgive your trespasses."

God will have no mercy on us if we recognize someone else's guilt and refuse to free them from shame by forgiving them. "Judge not, that you be not judged," Jesus said later in His Sermon. Don't spend time trying to remove a speck from someone else's eye when you have a plank in your own. Remember your own need, Jesus was saying. When we refuse to forgive, we are setting ourselves up as a judge and demanding that others be perfect—something we can't do. God will judge and demand perfection of us when we judge others.

When we forgive, we see through other people's behavior to their need. We recognize their guilt, and at the same time, see our own. We realize that we won't find justice in this world—it doesn't live here. So we give up the fruitless, heartbreaking search for it, and we give mercy to those who have wounded us.

I know of some who have limped into eternity with rope burns from the millstone of unforgiveness deep in their ankles. How do we cut the cord? In my case, I asked God to bless the girl who had wronged me. I asked Him to pull her close to His heart, believing that she had to be pretty miserable herself to lie about someone. I remembered my own need and was finally able to choose to forgive.

At times when I saw her my anger would stir up again, so I would once again lift her up to the throne of

grace and ask God to bless her. Only in remembering my own need for forgiveness could I choose to forgive. I didn't feel like forgiving. God chose to forgive and felt like it.

Inside Out

But you . . . who once were not a people but are
now the people of God, who had not obtained
mercy but now have obtained mercy.
1 Peter 2:9–10

*S*andra Cerda felt like she was a nobody. Her mother
abandoned her when Sandra was four years old. Her
grandparents took her in, but her grandfather began sexually abusing her and her life became a nightmare. Every
night she lay in bed, shivering, afraid and ashamed. She
longed to be loved, but felt unlovable and unclean.

At fifteen years old, with visions of that elusive white
picket fence and peaceful home, Sandra married. But her
dream was quickly dissipated. Her husband turned out
to be a violent man who constantly beat her. She finally
left him just after he beat her with a plank of wood when
she was three months pregnant. Once again, Sandra was
a nobody. She knew no one who had compassion or pity
on her.

Sandra found work as a topless dancer in a bar. She
longed for love and acceptance and looked for it in the

47

eyes of the men in the bar. Not finding the love she sought, Sandra decided to find a more respected profession.

Sandra began modeling for newspaper ads and commercials, a career in which she excelled. She eventually gained a coveted spot in a national swimsuit magazine. People were frequently complimenting her on her beauty. Yet, inside, she still felt ugly and alone. To stop the pain, Sandra began using crack cocaine, but it didn't change her identity—she was still a lost little girl. She had beautiful clothes and carefully applied makeup. But Sandra still felt she was a nobody.

A severe case of skin cancer changed Sandra's life. Sandra has shown me pictures of the infected skin that covered her body and left her unable to look at herself in the mirror. She received radiation treatment, but the cancer only grew worse. Sandra's doctors finally gave up on her. But before she gave up on herself, Sandra remembered a female relative who always seemed to have peace in her life. She was never as attractive as Sandra had been, but grace seemed to rest on her. So Sandra went to visit with her.

Sandra's relative not only revealed the source of peace in her life—God—but she told Sandra this same God longed to treat Sandra with kindness and compassion. Sandra wept as she heard about the love of Christ. She asked Him to forgive her for four abortions and a godless lifestyle.

All of her life Sandra had tried to fit in, to belong. She had looked unsuccessfully for acceptance in her family and through her work. She felt a glimmer of hope from

the approval she received because of her beauty, but the hope didn't keep her from feeling alone. And the cancer robbed her of the little hope she had.

Now, in her least attractive state, she who felt like a nobody became a somebody. When Sandra met the Lord, she discovered that He had chosen her and longed to show her His kindness. She had done nothing to attract His attention. She could do nothing to lose it. Sandra had been searching for a little pity. Instead, she found an identity, a sense of belonging, and a purpose for her life. She discovered that, as a believer, she was part of "a chosen generation, a royal priesthood, a holy nation, [God's] own special people," whose purpose was to proclaim God's praise. This, according to Peter in his first epistle, is the security all believers have.

Beauty is fragile and temporary. A life built on beauty alone will disappear as quickly as a home built of ice when the summer is coming. A life built on the love of God, however, will flourish and weather loneliness and trials because the love of God lasts forever.

God has completely healed Sandra. Her face is lovely again, but the beauty she exudes comes from the peace of knowing she has been found.

Grace and Big Bird

You therefore, my son, be strong in the grace that
is in Christ Jesus.
2 Timothy 2:1

I was on tour with my British band in the fall of 1983.
We had given sixty-three concerts in three months and I
was suffering from bus fever. A pastor in a small Kansas
town had asked if we could come and do a concert for
him after our Kansas City date. He told us that no one
ever came to his little town, so we said yes.

The night before the concert we arrived in this one-
horse town, exhausted. We pulled up to our motel—the
"Pheasant Shooters Inn"—and looked it over skepti-
cally, unsure of what we were in for. It far exceeded any
of our expectations—even with shoes on we stuck to the
carpet!

We were more prepared for the concert the next evening. The pastor had told us there would be only about
fifty people at the show, but they would be very appre-
ciative. And just as he said, at concert time, fifty people

came through the doors of the church. For some reason unknown to me, forty-nine of the people sat in the back three rows of the church, and in the front row, one man in a bright yellow T-shirt sat alone.

As I opened with the first song, I felt as if all the fruit of the Spirit had fallen off my tree. We sang our songs, and the forty-nine people in the back clapped politely. But "Big Bird" in the front never clapped once. I began to get annoyed. *Why does he have to sit in the front row if he's not going to clap?* I wondered. I decided that he had come to annoy me, and it was working. I began staring at him after songs trying to shame him into clapping, but he wouldn't respond.

When the concert was finally over, I sat in the pastor's study, bemused and self-pitying. Suddenly someone kicked the door. I opened it and there stood my adversary in yellow! He was smiling from ear to ear. "You will never know how much tonight has meant to me," he said. "I have all your albums, but I've asked God for a long time to bring you here." As I looked at this gracious, loving man, I realized that he had no arms.

I don't think I have ever been so ashamed in my whole life. In my need for approval, I had judged someone who had faithfully prayed for me for years. I had judged him based only on what I could see.

As I lay in my freezing cold waterbed at the "Pheasant Shooters Inn" that night, I asked God to forgive me. And then I asked myself some questions. "What if the man had arms and was genuinely there to annoy me? Would that have given me an excuse for rejecting him?"

Not if I was going to respond with grace. Grace is unmerited favor; grace gives mercy and love when we don't deserve it.

The Hebrew word for *grace* means "to bend, or stoop." Donald Barnhouse, the late pastor and Bible scholar, painted a beautiful picture of grace when he said, "Love that goes upward is worship, love that goes outward is affection, love that stoops is grace." When we didn't deserve it, God stooped down by becoming a Man to love us. I needed to stoop down from my place on the stage, from my needs, to love the man in my audience.

One of the best books I've ever read is *The Grace Awakening,* by Chuck Swindoll. I wish that it was mandatory reading for every believer. It is a book of life, of freedom, of the overwhelming grace of God.

Chuck came on "Heart to Heart" to discuss the book and told a story similar to mine. While he was speaking at a conference, he was distracted by a man who kept falling asleep during his sessions. Finally, after the last session, the man's wife approached Chuck. He straightened his back and placed his hands on his hips, preparing himself to accept the woman's apology for her husband's behavior.

Instead of offering an apology, however, the woman reached out and shook Chuck's hand warmly and thanked him for his messages. Her husband was dying of cancer, she told Chuck. His medication made him drowsy at times, but he wouldn't miss Chuck's sessions for the world.

The woman continued talking as Chuck's shoulders slowly sank.

It is easy to judge quickly when we see only what is before our eyes. But when we look at others with the grace Christ has shown us, we can see beyond the outer shell to the human heart. As Paul said in 2 Corinthians 5:16, "we regard no one according to the flesh" because of the grace of Christ in reconciling us to God. Now we can have the patience to try to understand what is happening inside others and love them so they can be reconciled to God too.

Our churches and our witness to the world would be transformed if we could extend this mercy and love to ourselves and then to each other.

My Heart Trusted in Him and I Am Helped

> The Lord is my strength and my shield;
> My heart trusted in Him, and I am helped;
> Therefore my heart greatly rejoices,
> And with my song I will praise Him.
> Psalm 28:7

"Oh, thank the Lord, it's Friday." My secretary, Laura, sat back in her chair with a sigh, looking forward to a quiet weekend with friends.

I found it hard to share her jubilation. It was the end of my work week at CBN, but the beginning of my weekend concert schedule. Friday night, Newark, Delaware; Saturday, Bismarck, North Dakota. All week long my friends at work had been coming down with the flu, and when I had awakened that morning I knew that it had hit me too. Sniffling, I gathered together my papers and books for the following week's shows so that I could prepare for them on my long flights and trudged out the door of the office.

As I drove to the airport, I felt empty; I began to wonder how much longer I could keep going with this crazy schedule! A car pulled out in front of me and I angrily sounded my horn, grateful that I didn't have a "Smile God loves you!" bumper sticker.

When Norman met me at the gate, he could tell I was not in the mood for idle chatter, so he picked up his *Time* magazine and began to read. I wanted to tell him that I couldn't keep going, that I felt like a rag doll, but I couldn't find the words. Norman has always been a hard worker, and when I've tried to keep up, I've felt caught up in a wave more powerful than I. I was wondering that day when the wave would dump me on the shore, useless and spent.

We landed in Philadelphia and drove to Newark. As I stood on stage that night, I had the strangest feeling of unreality. I felt as if I were trapped inside a goldfish bowl and I couldn't touch anyone.

When I awoke the next morning my head hurt and my throat was sore. I looked at my pale reflection in the merciless bathroom mirror and sighed.

Within hours Norman and I were on yet another plane to Bismarck. Throughout the flight I prayed for the right words to tell Norman how I felt.

"Ladies and gentlemen, please fasten your seat belts, we're about to land in Bismarck."

Taking a deep breath, I turned to Norman. "Norman, I don't want you to give me a yes or no on this, I just want you to listen and think and pray about it.

"I feel as if I'm at a crossroads in my life and I need to choose a new direction. I can't go on living like this."

Norman looked at me and saw the tears in my eyes. He put his hand over mine. "Maybe this is God's timing, Sheila. Maybe we should rethink our direction."

We got off the plane and there standing in front of us was Dick Mills. Dick is a wonderful man, a gifted Bible teacher, and a true prophet. He took hold of us and said, "Now, about this change of direction. God is in this. You have been faithful to Him and you are about to experience a breakthrough in your lives and ministry."

You could have knocked me down with a feather! It was as if he had heard every word of our conversation. I still don't know what he was doing in Bismarck, North Dakota, but I know that God sent him to speak to us.

David wrote of a similar experience in Psalm 28. He, too, cried out to God for help. And he pleaded with God not to be silent in response to his requests. We may find it hard to endure when people misunderstand us or have left us alone, but the ultimate loneliness comes if we feel as if the God of the universe cannot or will not hear us.

The tone of the psalm changes when David believes God has heard his prayers. Suddenly he is shouting happily: "Blessed be the LORD." He doesn't say exactly what has happened that makes him know God has heard him. But knowing God has heard his prayers enables him to sing God's praise.

God is not a brutal taskmaster, determined to sap our strength. He is a loving, caring father, who'll even send a busy man to North Dakota to tell us that everything is going to be all right.

In a House Called Hope

"And whoever gives one of these little ones only a cup of cold water in the name of a disciple, assuredly, I say to you, he shall by no means lose his reward."
Matthew 10:42

*A*s co-host of the Christian Broadcasting Network's "700 Club" I get to meet people like Sara Trollinger, founder and president of House of Hope Ministries. This full-time residential center shelters girls aged twelve through eighteen from the streets of central Florida.

I heard of Sara through a friend and was anxious to interview this fascinating woman. After I met her on my turf, I wanted to see her ministry with my own eyes. So, in January 1991, Norman and I flew down to spend a weekend with Sara and her "family."

When Norman and I arrived at House of Hope, we were greeted by a tall, elegant lady, with a warm, welcoming smile and shoulders soft enough to absorb a

thousand tears. Little lines around Sara's eyes told of hard work, sleepless nights, and laughter.

Sara showed us into the den, where the girls streamed in to say hello. Dressed in anything from blue jeans to pretty dresses, the girls looked lovely. They sang a song, which had been written especially for them and visited with us for a while. Then they departed, and we had supper with Sara.

As we ate, Sara told us some of the girls' stories. Many of them had arrived at the house, addicted to drugs or alcohol, rebellion or hopelessness written all over their faces. Many had been sexually abused or raped. One girl had tried to hang herself with the strap of her mother's purse in order to escape her grandfather's sexual assaults.

For six years, Sara has greeted these girls at her door, hugging them and telling them they are special. Most girls initially shy away from this, unsure of how to respond to genuine care. Through the weeks or months they stay in the House of Hope, however, the girls find hope and love through Sara and a personal relationship with Jesus.

When Jesus commissioned His disciples to go out into the world, He said that those who received the disciples because of Jesus would be receiving Jesus. And whoever gave a cup of cold water to another person in the name of a disciple would not lose his reward. A seemingly insignificant act—giving someone a cup of cold water—was considered worthy of reward when it was done for Jesus' sake. In Matthew 18:5, we read Jesus' words, "And whoever receives one little child like this in My name receives Me." The least acts done for the "least" of those

Jesus loves have the same magnitude as that of receiving Christ Himself into our homes and entertaining Him.

Sara works long, hard hours with girls many consider the "least," but she knows that when she reaches out in Jesus' name to "the least of these," she touches the heart of God.

Here are the words of the girls' song:

> In a house called hope
> There's a love that never gives up
> In a house called hope
> There's a peace that's hard to
> interrupt.
>
> Though the devil keeps trying
> Don't you know that he's lying
> The Lord always wins in the end
> 'Cause Jesus lives and gives in
> A house called hope.

A Refuge in Troubled Times

> God is our refuge and strength,
> A very present help in trouble.
> Psalm 46:1

I was talking with Sandi Patti and Larnelle Harris one fall day, as a coach was taking us to an evening concert where we were to perform. Sandi sat up with a shout and pointed out the window. I scanned the horizon for a three-legged cow, a U.F.O., a Billy Graham crusade. Sandi had spotted a Wal-Mart! We decided Sandi's enthusiasm for Wal-Marts was well shared across the country, given the $32 billion in business they did in 1990.

A few months later I sat and listened to the story of Ruth Glass, a beautifully groomed elegant woman who is the wife of the C.E.O. of Wal-Mart.

When she was eight years old, Ruth was taken from bar to bar, throughout Albuquerque, New Mexico, by her alcoholic parents. She felt unloved and unlovely. At age fifteen, she married David Glass, hoping that marriage would fill the empty place in her heart.

The young couple struggled financially, sometimes sleeping in their car, sometimes on a mat on a cold floor. But David was a dreamer and was determined to work to realize those dreams.

Together they put David through college. Then one good job begat another. As he became more successful, Ruth's insecurities rose to the surface. Having gained some weight with the birth of her two children, she began to take diet pills that had been prescribed for her by her doctor. Soon she needed more and more. Eventually, she was taking thirty-two pills a day. Ruth realized that she was out of control, so she stopped taking them—she went "cold turkey"—but the emptiness remained. Ruth then began to drink—a glass of wine before she left for an evening, a couple of glasses when she arrived at her destination, and a glass when she came home.

As she sat in her room one afternoon, having drunk all day, David came in and stood over her. He looked her in the face and turned and left with the children. Ruth knew she had become everything she despised in her parents— an out of control drunk.

The afternoon faded into evening and gradually a plan unfolded in her mind. There was a long winding cliff-top road near the Glasses' home, and Ruth decided she would drive off it. She would make it look like an accident, of course. David would remarry; the children would have a new mother who would love and care for them; there would be no ugly divorce, no loose ends.

As Ruth told me of her plans to kill herself, I was chilled by her carefully thought-out reasoning. In her mind it was the most loving thing to do.

The next few days, Ruth stayed in her room, numb to the passage of time. She finally flicked on the television and heard a voice telling her Jesus loved her. Arrested by these words, Ruth cried out for God to save her. She knew this was her last chance to get help. As she prayed, a peace and a joy she had never known began to swell inside her heart. And Ruth knew without a shadow of a doubt that she had come face-to-face with the God of the universe.

Each day after that Ruth Glass sat down with her Bible, a glass of wine, and a cigarette, and read and re-read the gospels. She had no idea of how a Christian should live; she just wanted to know more about this Jesus Who loved her. One day she noticed that, after she had been there for hours, the wine glass was still full. God had healed her heart. She didn't need alcohol any-more.

Ruth gave up on herself, and God became her refuge and her strength, a very present help in trouble.

Psalm 46:6–7 says that nations may rage and king-doms may be moved, but God's voice melts the earth. Nothing can stand against the power of God. He makes wars cease—wars that rage around us and wars of fears and insecurities that rage against our souls. "Be still," the psalmist wrote, "and know that I am God" (v. 10). When we are still, we will see God's works and strength. We will see, just as Ruth Glass did, that God has been with us all along, and He wants to heal us so we can serve Him.

Today, Ruth travels the country, telling others of the

love of God. Some hide their loneliness behind exquisitely tailored suits, some drown their pain with pills and alcohol. Ruth is able to tell them that God is not a distant benevolent old man, but He is a very present help in times of trouble.

My Name Is Sheila, and I'm a Sinner

> But if we walk in the light as He is in the light, we
> have fellowship with one another, and the blood
> of Jesus Christ His Son cleanses us from all sin.
> 1 John 1:7

I sat anxiously by the phone, waiting for news from my friend. The ring shook the air and sent me jumping out of my chair. I picked up the receiver.

"How did it go?" I asked.

One of my best friends had recently joined Alcoholics Anonymous after struggling for a long time on his own, getting nowhere. I was glad he was finally getting some help. But I was nervous too. Would they understand him? Would he feel accepted?

"Sheila," he answered, "for the first time in my life, I realize what the church could be."

"What do you mean?"

"Well, I stood up, told them my name, told them I had

a problem, and they understood and accepted me. The room was filled with people who knew they couldn't make it on their own. We needed each other."

I was happy my friend had begun the long journey home. But I was also intrigued by his comments. God's Word teaches us that when we are weak, then we are strong. So we should be most free to admit our needs in church. But instead, so often, we feel obliged to sit in church, grinning like Cheshire cats so we will be "good witnesses."

The world is not looking for Stepford Christians, for those who seem to have had a personality lobotomy. People are tired of pretense. We struggle with failures; we long for intimacy. So why are we feigning perfection before God and one another?

Perhaps it is because we misread passages like James 5:16: "Confess your trespasses to one another, and pray for one another, that you may be healed. The effective, fervent prayer of a righteous man avails much." We think "righteous man" means "superhero." So we search for the super religious person who can save the day—or attempt to be that person ourselves.

When we do this we miss the truth that confessing our trespasses and praying for one another makes us the "righteous men" who can bring about healing from God. We become righteous by admitting our weaknesses to each other, and we gain healing and strength through their prayers. When we try to become superheroes, we become more deeply entrenched in our failures rather than find healing.

I was surprised, a couple of years ago, by an onslaught of letters from believing women who claimed their husbands abused them.

> "Sheila, my husband is an elder in our church, but he beats me. Please help me."
>
> "I know that I have to submit to my husband, but he makes me feel so worthless. What can I do?"
>
> "My husband is so determined to control me. I feel as if I am disappearing. I feel alone."

I had only recently rejected material for a program on men who abuse women, thinking the topic irrelevant for our audience.

I invited Dr. Margaret Rincke to be a guest on my show and to respond to this issue. Dr. Rincke told me that this little-talked-about issue was a much greater problem than the church wanted to admit. Women feared coming forward for help, thinking they wouldn't be believed or feeling they should suffer in order to "lay up treasure in heaven." Men refused to admit their behavior, believing they needed to maintain the appearance of perfection and control.

The picture was distressing. Men and women were suffering daily. People needed healing and support. Yet, everyone was hiding the truth, seemingly because Christians don't have such problems.

Like James, John proclaimed the freedom and healing that would come from confession of sin. "If we walk in the light as He is in the light, we have fellowship with one another, and the blood of Jesus Christ His Son

cleanses us from all sin. If we say that we have no sin, we deceive ourselves, and the truth is not in us. If we confess our sins, He is faithful and just to forgive us our sins and to cleanse us from all unrighteousness" (1 John 1:7–9).

Walking in the light means we are cleansed by the blood of Christ and able to have fellowship with other believers. We will be constantly cleansed, wrote John, if we confess our sins as they surface. When we hide our sins and cover our weaknesses, when we pretend to be Christian Supermen, we live in denial—"the truth is not in us." We then become isolated from one another and from God.

Can you imagine what freedom would come to the body of Christ if we could stand up and say, "Hello, I'm Sheila, and I'm a sinner. I need your help to make it." In 1992 I have begun to receive counseling to help me deal with my father's death. For too long, I have filled the ache with noise and service. But I'm ready to take off the bandages and allow fresh air and sunlight to touch my wounds. I'm ready to admit I need help. I'm ready to lay down my pride and acknowledge I can't heal my own pain. It's hard to be exposed as flawed and imperfect, but a wound that's bandaged forever will never heal.

It's hard to admit our helplessness over our behavior and to ask for help. But I don't want to live in the chains of pride and fear. I want to find healing and to share life with other believers. Admitting our need for help from being victims or abusers or addicts or hypocrites can free us and the generations to come. I want to live with real people. And I want to be real too.

Perhaps some of us walk with a limp. Perhaps we will always have scars. The One we follow has carried His scars for a long time, and He longs for us to show Him ours so He can heal them.

Love That Doesn't Give Up

And let us not grow weary while doing good, for in due season we shall reap if we do not lose heart.
Galatians 6:9

*J*ohn Shelton stood in court and listened as he was sentenced to two consecutive life terms in a mental facility for the criminally insane. As he was led away, he cursed God. "This isn't what I turned myself in for, God. You've turned on me!"

John Shelton had never known love from a person, much less from God. He was raised in an abusive home by an alcoholic mother who made her living as a prostitute. She married for the first time when she was eleven years old, and again six times after that. From the time he was six years old until he was twelve, John was sexually abused by a close female relative. When he was eight years old, he was raped by his uncle who had just been released from prison. The abuse continued for several nights until John got the courage to tell his mother. She

then attacked her brother with an iron skillet and almost killed him.

For John, the nightmare lived on outside his home. At school, the other children nicknamed him "the termite" because he was short. He felt alone and afraid.

"By the time I was a young adult," says John, "my inner rage had reached a boiling point." He felt as if the world owed him and he set out to take revenge. He bought a .44-caliber Magnum and began a brutal spree of robbery and rape. He felt as if he was in control for the first time in his life.

Early one August morning, John broke into a home with the intention of robbing and assaulting the woman who lived there alone. He went up to her room where she was asleep, pointed his gun at her head, and told her to do whatever he asked. Much to John's amazement, the woman opened her eyes and calmly replied, "Sir, you can do anything you want temporarily to my mind; you can do something temporarily to my body; but praise God, you can't touch my spirit!"

The woman then leapt out of bed and began to thank God for sending this needy young man to her home. John dropped his gun in surprise. The woman scooped up the gun and told him to follow her—she was going to fix him some breakfast. After they had eaten and John had gotten up to leave, she hugged him and told him that God had a master plan for his life. Motivated to change the direction of his life, John went straight from her home to the police station to turn himself in, never expecting he would be sentenced to two life terms in prison.

The mental facility where John was sent was bleak and depressing. His anger and his feeling that he had been betrayed by God festered each day he was there.

One day a tall, well-built man with a perpetual smile came to see John. He introduced himself as John Misko, and he told Shelton that he had come to tell him of God's love. Shelton's first thought was that he was in prison because of one religious nut—he had no intentions of listening to another. But Misko wouldn't go away. For five years he visited Shelton, withstanding his constant abuse and swearing.

Nothing in John Shelton's life spoke of a God of peace and love like the lady who refused to be afraid and the man who refused to stop loving him. These two people did not get tired or give up, even when their physical bodies and personal dignity were being threatened.

The apostle Paul understood threats and persecution. He chronicled his experiences and those of his companions in 2 Corinthians 4:8–9: "We are hard pressed on every side, yet not crushed; we are perplexed, but not in despair; persecuted, but not forsaken; struck down, but not destroyed." Neither Paul nor his companions gave up amidst their sufferings. They rejoiced, knowing that Christ's life was being seen through their lives and that others were coming to know Christ because of their sufferings. They also held on to the hope that one day they and the ones they loved would be with Jesus forever (v. 14). And so would John Shelton.

After five years of being visited by John Misko, Shelton got down on his knees and asked Christ to set him free of the prison inside his heart. He asked the Lord

to help him forgive those who had wounded him and to forgive him for wounding so many others.

Many people in our world today are filled with rage and hatred. As we hang on to the hope of everlasting life with God, we will reach beyond our barriers of safety to love others. And we will begin to see that even the most calloused heart can be transformed by unrelenting love.

Jesus on Skid Row

For as the body without the spirit is dead, so faith
without works is dead also.
James 2:26

"When visitors drop by at mealtime, never ask if
they've had dinner," Willie Jordan's mom used to say. "If
they haven't they might be too embarrassed to admit it.
Always say, 'You'll join us for dinner, won't you?' "

Willie Jordan was raised by godly parents who had
little money but a lot of love. Her mother's door was
always open to her neighbors, and they knew they
would find a welcome and a simple hot meal there. Willie has taken those lessons learned as a child to the streets
of Los Angeles. When she was twenty-three years old,
she married Fred Jordan and their shared commitment to
helping others drew them together with Fred Jordan
Missions, which had been established in 1944 on skid
row in Los Angeles.

Willie described her marriage to Fred as "magic, pure
magic." They never fell out of love.

On April 4, 1988, Fred suffered a massive heart attack

and was hospitalized. Willie felt she would fall apart when he died—she was certain she would want to retire from the ministry. But as she stood in her husband's hospital room, watching him take his last breath, she felt God reach out and grab hold of her. Willie became aware of the power and the presence of God as she hadn't been since the day she was born again when she was thirteen years old.

With the Lord's strength and joy, Willie assumed the mantle of leadership for the Fred Jordan Mission. And today the mission serves more than two thousand meals a day to poor and homeless people and sleeps two hundred and fifty people a night. It also provides job training programs, child care services, and family, marriage, and job counseling services.

In his letter to the church, James wrote of the importance of having both faith and works. "For as the body without the spirit is dead, so faith without works is dead also." Works give life to faith the way the spirit gives life to the body. James called believers to show mercy actively to everyone—not just a select few—because God was not select in showing us mercy. How can we do this? Through our works—by giving the same honor to the poor and the wealthy, by providing food and clothing for those in need.

Willie told me of finding a woman and her five children living in a garbage sack behind a McDonald's restaurant. The mother was going through the trash, looking for something to give to her children to eat. (Over forty percent of the nation's homeless are women and children, who survive from day to day, afraid of be-

ing raped or beaten.) "Homeless mothers feel the same love for their children," Willie said. "They have the same needs, the same desire for their children to be strong, healthy, and happy. The only difference is that they don't dare to dream. I'm here to give them a dream."

I would imagine many of us are held back by fear. We are afraid to reach out to those who are different from us, as if they are an alien form of life. But with such faith as Willie's, we can see that people have the same needs, and we can show everyone the same mercy.

My friend Brennan Manning travels across the U.S. speaking on the relentless passionate love of God in Christ. One evening he encountered a homeless drunk on skid row who asked him for money to buy wine. Brennan got down on his knees and took this man's dirty hands in his and kissed them. Tears rolled down the man's cheeks. He didn't really want wine; he wanted to be loved. Brennan took him to a detoxification unit where he dried out and began to live again.

When God looked at our sin-stained world, He could have washed His hands of us, but He sent Jesus to bend down and touch us and make us clean. He does not offer us His love based on our appearance or our social status. Instead, Christ looks at each one of us and mends our broken hearts so we can turn around and kiss someone's feet and let them know that they are loved.

An Inch from the Gates of Hell

> You are of God, little children, and have overcome them, because He who is in you is greater than he who is in the world.
> 1 John 4:4

*W*hen I was sixteen years old, I asked the headmaster of my school if I could show the movie "The Cross and the Switchblade" at lunchtime to all 1600 students. I was excited when he gave me permission. I was the only Christian that I knew of in the student body, and I felt that the story of this film would change lives.

The day we showed the movie the auditorium was packed. As the story began to unfold, you could have heard a pin drop. Unfortunately, I had never seen anyone inject themselves with drugs, so when it got to that part, I fainted and was carried out by Mr. Lunam, the biology teacher!

Years later, I met Nicky Cruz, the main character of the movie, when I interviewed him. Nicky was the eighth son in a family who practiced black magic and witchcraft in Puerto Rico. His parents believed in good and bad demonic spirits and felt that they were in touch with the good ones. His father, Yelo Cruz, called "the Great One," was a rural healer who communicated with powerful spirits. He expected Nicky to follow in his footsteps.

As a two-month old baby, Nicky almost died of a strange fever. Torn with grief, his father took his wife's best black hen and began to chant and cast a spell. Suddenly, he chopped off the hen's head and let the blood spill over his son. Nicky lived. But his mother began to believe that he was evil. When he was eight years old, she told him she hated him. "You have been cursed from the day you were born," she said. "You are not my son; you are the son of Satan." Nicky lost all feeling that day—he never cried again during his childhood.

When Nicky was fifteen years old, his father took him to the airport, gave him a ten-dollar bill and a plane ticket to New York, and wished him a better life. In New York, Nicky fell in with a street gang called the Mau Maus, and he continued his life of violence and hatred. Often as he lay in bed at night, though thousands of miles away from his home, he was still haunted by his mother's words, "You are the son of Satan."

One day a skinny preacher walked up to Nicky, looked him straight in the eyes, and said, "Nicky, Jesus loves you." Nicky was enraged. No one loved him—no one had ever loved him. He determined to kill the preacher, but there was something about this man that he couldn't fight. Nicky went to an evening church service with a gun in his pocket, bent on blowing David Wilkerson away. When David saw Nicky enter the

church, he began to pray aloud for Nicky. God melted Nicky's heart, and he began to cry out to God to forgive him. For the first time in his life he knew that he was loved, he was not a mistake. He began working on the streets with Dave, sharing his new life with friends and rival gang members.

Nicky's brother, Frank, who was also living in New York, bumped into Nicky one day. "Mama's searching for you. She's dying, Nicky," said Frank. Bitterness and hatred toward this woman who had cursed him overwhelmed Nicky. But he knew in his heart that he had to forgive her. He flew home to Puerto Rico, apprehensive about the spiritual battle ahead. His father and brothers met him at the airport, friendly, but distant, trying to sense if his power was greater than theirs. When Nicky saw his mother, he was shocked. She was old and thin and deathly ill.

Nicky escaped from the house for a while and made his way to the local church where the congregation had met for prayer. He asked the pastor if he and some of the other believers would come to his house that night and pray for his mother. "I'll never enter that evil-spirited house," a church member cried out. But the pastor understood and agreed to come.

Nicky bought his mother a new dress that afternoon and took it home to her. He helped her put on the dress and then washed her face and combed her hair. He carried her to the living room sofa and as they sat there he heard a noise coming up the hill. Nicky rushed to the window and saw 500 Christians coming toward the house with guitars and tamborines, singing the praise of

Jesus. Nicky's father slipped away and hid in the forest behind the house. But that night Nicky's mom was gloriously saved and healed. She lived for another twenty-five years!

When Nicky's father was almost eighty years old, he lay in a hospital, weak and afraid. "All my life I have served lying and deceiving spirits. If I try to call on the name of the Lord now, they will kill me." Nicky assured his father that the One that he loved and served is greater and stronger than the one who is in the world. He told him not to be afraid.

Finally, one day, Yelo Cruz told his son, "I've made my choice. I'm going to give my life to Jesus and I'm going to ask Him to take me then." He prayed a simple, fervent prayer, and a glorious peace illuminated his face. Eight hours later, he died. He found salvation at the very gates of hell.

Nicky told me that he often wonders what kind of man his father would have been if he had met Christ as a young man. Yelo Cruz wasted his life in the service of the destroyer. In his last days, the powers he had served all his life turned on him; yet, Yelo discovered the truth those who love Jesus know: When God's spirit is in you, the very gates of hell cannot prevail against you.

Love Never Fails

Love . . . bears all things, believes all things, hopes
all things, endures all things. Love never fails.
1 Corinthians 13:7–8

*S*am Huddleston stood with tears rolling down his
cheeks as he watched his mother walk away from her
marriage and her family. A little boy, he couldn't understand what was happening. All he knew was that his
momma was gone and his daddy was left to raise him
and his two brothers and three sisters by himself. A seed
of bitterness took root in Sam's heart the day his mom
disappeared, and the seed grew each passing year.

In high school, Sam's friends began drinking sloe gin
and he joined in to be part of the crowd. He got so drunk
the first time he tried it, he felt as if his shoes were coming out of his head. Sam's daddy, a devout Christian
man, understood his son's pain and committed to help
him be faithful to God. At night he would ask Sam,
"Have you prayed for your momma today?" But Sam
had no time for his father's God, and he got deeper and
deeper in trouble.

One morning Sam came to from an all-night drinking binge in someone else's home. He turned over in bed and vaguely took in the face of the young girl asleep beside him. He heard someone knocking on a door somewhere, and he wished the person would go away. Suddenly, two police officers appeared by his bed and told him to get up and put his pants on; he was under arrest.

What did I do? Sam wondered as he sat, handcuffed in the squad car. *What could I have done?* He had no memory of the night before.

At the police station he was told that he and his cousin had burst into a liquor store, robbed it, and killed the store owner.

At seventeen, Sam Huddleston found himself in prison, sentenced to five years to life. As he lay in his cell that night, alone and afraid, he wondered if his daddy would come to see him. He felt ashamed for the disgrace he had brought on the Huddleston name. The next day his daddy did come to see him. "Son," he said, "we're in trouble. I don't know what we're going to do, but we'll make it with God's help."

Sam soon discovered that the law of the jungle ruled in prison. It was survival of the fittest. Daily there were knife fights, rapes. The only time he felt safe was in his cell at night. And then he was haunted in his sleep by the screams of the liquor store owner, "Please don't kill me, don't stab me anymore."

One day as Sam sat alone in the prison courtyard in utter despair, he remembered something his father had once said to him: "Son, if you're ever alone and I can't get to you, call on Jesus. He'll be there." Sam called out

to the Lord saying, "I don't believe in You, but my daddy says You're real and he's never lied to me. If You can hear my prayer, please change my life."

That night he lay down in his cell and slept peacefully for the first night since the murder. He still had to serve his years in prison, and it was tough to live out his faith in front of his fellow inmates. But he knew that God was real. As his friends began to see a difference in him, many of them wanted to find the peace that he had found.

Sam Huddleston appeared on my show and told me his experiences. "You know, Sheila," he said, "a lot of people are skeptical of prison salvations. They think we had nothing else to turn to in prison, and when we get out, we'll change our minds. But prison didn't change my life; Jesus did."

The day Sam was released from prison his daddy was waiting for him. His father ran to Sam, hugged him, and took him home. That evening as they sat at the dinner table, Sam's father took a piece of paper out of a drawer. It was a note that Sam had written to him years ago, telling him that he wanted nothing to do with him or his God. "Why did you keep it, daddy?" Sam asked. "Because, son, I knew someday we would burn it together." Huddleston never gave up on his boy. He always hoped, always trusted. A friend once told him that if Sam were his son, he would have given up on him years ago. Sam's father replied, "He's not your son, he's my son, and I'll never give up on him."

Jesus told a story of a son whose father never gave up on him. The son took his inheritance and left the village where he had grown up to have his own way in the

world. According to the tradition of the culture, the father should have considered the son dead when the son left, and he should never have allowed the son to return. But instead, Jesus said, "when he was still a great way off, his father saw him and had compassion, and ran and fell on his neck and kissed him" (Luke 15:20). The father hadn't given up on his son. He had never considered his son dead. He was waiting, watching for his son to return. He embraced his son publicly, unashamed, and even threw a party for him!

Our heavenly Father looks at us the same way. We can pack our bags, say we're tired, shake our fist at God, and walk away. But His love for us never fails. He waits for us; He watches to see when we will return. And when we do, He embraces us openly and is not ashamed of us.

The night Sam was released from prison, he and his father took a match to the note Sam had written years before, and watched its words become engulfed in flames. When it was gone, all that was left at the table was a father and his son and a love that never fails.

God's Plans

For I know the thoughts that I think toward you,
says the LORD, thoughts of peace and not of evil,
to give you a future and a hope.
Jeremiah 29:11

On April 15, 1992, Gianna Jesson was fifteen years old. That's the day she has chosen to celebrate as her birthday, though she was never born. Gianna was aborted.

When Gianna's birth mother was six months pregnant, she decided to have a saline abortion. No one expected the live birth of a struggling two-pound baby girl. A member of the clinical staff realized that Gianna was a live birth, so she placed Gianna in an incubator and transferred her to a hospital. The hours Gianna spent in her mother's womb, gulping the toxic salt solution left her crippled with cerebral palsy and spinal bifida. In Gianna's words, she "looked like a piece of cooked spaghetti" when she was born.

Gianna remained in critical condition for three months. Believing she wouldn't live a year, her doctors

placed her in a foster home for high-risk children. But God had other plans for a home for Gianna.

At the foster home, a woman named Penny cared for Gianna. She took this helpless baby home one day, and her daughter, Dianna DePaul, fell in love with Gianna. Shortly after that, Dianna adopted her.

I first saw Gianna on television at a press conference, representing the pro-life cause. She came across as a vivacious, intelligent, loving girl, who held no grudge against her birth mother. She told reporters that anyone who had had an abortion needed compassion not judgment. She publicly thanked God for her life, saying God must have a plan for her life because she was alive when she should have been dead.

I wanted to meet this amazing girl, so I contacted Dianna DePaul, and asked Dianna and Gianna to be guests on "Heart to Heart." A few weeks later we sat together in the studio. Gianna exuded joy and vitality, even as she talked about the humiliation she felt when the children at school would laugh at her. "I would run home and ask my Mom why God would do this to me. I would cry, and my Mom would tell me that God had a special plan for my life."

Dianna shared her experience of mothering this unique young woman. She revealed the surprise she had the day she finally decided she had to tell Gianna the circumstances of her birth. Gianna was twelve years old and had asked Dianna why she was disabled. Dianna prepared herself to answer by asking Gianna to sit down. But before she could begin, Gianna piped up, "I was aborted, wasn't I?" Dianna fell speechless as Gianna

added, "At least I have an interesting reason for my disability. Now I will do what God has for me to do."

Although she was only twelve years old, Gianna had an assurance from God, deep in her heart, that He was caring for her. A plan had been put into action to destroy her life, but Gianna believed God had intervened and that He had done so for a purpose—to give her a future and a hope. She had learned from Dianna and through her suffering to trust God's plans, that they were not meant for evil.

Gianna lives to speak on behalf of the unborn. She reaches out compassionately, as well, to women who have aborted their children and are torn with guilt. She offers them the peace she has found in knowing God that God's plans for life cannot be thwarted. Gianna can tell them and everyone that God's plans are not simply about survival. They are about peace and hope.

Going Home

So when this corruptible has put on incorruption, and this mortal has put on immortality, then shall be brought to pass the saying that is written: "Death is swallowed up in victory."
1 Corinthians 15:54

*M*y grandfather had Alzheimer's disease. It was a nightmare for my grandmother and my mother to watch this respected, hard-working man become, at times, a helpless stranger. He would wander off into the streets outside his home, hopelessly disoriented. The disease affected his personality, too, so he would be troublesome and impossible to please. My mother felt as if her parent had become her child. She left school when she was only fifteen, despite her academic promise, to help my grandmother cope.

One day I talked with Elisabeth Elliot about a helpful, practical book she has written, called *Forget Me Not*. (You may remember Elisabeth as the wife of missionary Jim Elliot, who was killed by the Auca Indians in Ecuador.) The book deals with what she learned in caring for her

elderly parent. She talks about the inner turmoil she felt, trying to make the right decisions for this beloved parent, who was at one time a strong, independent thinker. She sensed the frustration and helplessness that plagued her mother, and she talks of the guilt and weariness that tore at her own soul.

Elisabeth told me we should not be crushed when those we love, who are old and frail and confined, seem discontent and critical of whatever we do to try to help them. What they are longing for can't be found down here. They want to go home. We need to do what we feel is the best and right thing, offering family care at home whenever possible. If that is not an option, we can find a good, loving nursing home.

It's hard to watch someone we love suffer. It's hard to watch once capable, alert people begin to wither and fade like fragile leaves in the fall. But when our journey down here no longer fills us with hope and joy, we can hang on to the hope Paul gave the Corinthians— that there is a resurrection, there is life after death. We can know that just beyond our sight stands a choir singing:

O Death, where is your sting?
O Hades, where is your victory? . . .
[T]hanks be to God, who gives us the victory through our Lord Jesus Christ (1 Cor. 15:55, 57).

We must hold on to the promise that even death itself will be swallowed up in the victory of everlasting life.

Our physical bodies which, Paul said, were "sown in corruption," will be "raised in incorruption. . . . in glory." In heaven "there shall be no more death, nor sorrow, nor crying; and there shall be no more pain, for the former things have passed away. . . . 'Behold, I make all things new'" (Rev. 21:4–5). Our fragile bodies will be restored and perfected, and we will live forever.

Because of this hope, we can know that our "labor is not in vain in the Lord" (1 Cor. 15:58). We can bear the grief of seeing our loved ones experience pain or death without being overwhelmed or disillusioned. We can hold on to our faith through pain because we are looking forward to the day when we will be made new and we will be together with those we love in heaven.

I sat on the boardwalk at Laguna Beach in California recently and wrote this:

> Are you tired from the journey
> Are your feet heavy and sore
> Are you longing for the homeland
> And loved ones who wait upon the shore?
>
> Can you hear a distant drummer
> Play an old familiar song
> Giving strength now to the weary
> Telling us that it won't be long.
>
> I'm going home
> Will you come with me
> No longer walk this earth alone

> There is a rest beyond the sorrow
> And for the pilgrim, there's a home.

It is good to remember that the Shepherd loves His sheep, and gently carries the broken, helpless ones.

Dry Cleaning for the Mind

> For though we walk in the flesh, we do not war
> according to the flesh. . . . casting down argu-
> ments and every high thing that exalts itself
> against the knowledge of God, bringing every
> thought into captivity to the obedience of Christ.
> 2 Corinthians 10:3, 5

*T*hey said it was inevitable. I never believed it would
happen. But it did. I turned thirty-five!

I woke up that birthday morning, crawled out of bed,
switched on the merciless bathroom light, and took in-
ventory. A few little lines around my eyes. A healthy
sprinkling of grey only Debbie, my hairstylist, and I
know about (hate that grey, wash it away!). I took my
wedding picture off the shelf and compared the bride
with the woman in the mirror. All in all I had to con-
clude that, like a fine old cheese, I had improved with
age. Convinced I had a few good years left, I went
downstairs for breakfast.

As I ate my oatmeal, I read a disturbing statistic in the
newspaper: 75 to 80 percent of men aged 35 to 55 expe-

rience a moderate to severe midlife crisis. The figures for women were not quite so high, but still fairly substantial. I can hear you say, "Yes, but we are Christians; this won't happen to us!" And I say, "Yeah, and I live next door to the Easter Bunny!"

Dr. Paul Mickey has written a funny and helpful book called *Breaking Away from Wedlock Deadlock*. Couples take great pride, Dr. Mickey says in his book, in not having committed adultery; yet, they commit emotional adultery every day. A few years ago former President Jimmy Carter told *Playboy* magazine that he struggled with sexual fantasies. (I read this account in Dr. Mickey's book—not in the magazine!) This is one way of committing emotional adultery. But anytime we regard possessions or jobs or other interests more highly than we do our mates, we commit emotional adultery.

As Christians, we may feel safe playing this game of emotional adultery. But in fact, playing along weakens our defenses. Our thoughts set the course for our actions. Often, we eventually live out in our physical world what we think about most. That is why Paul warned believers in Corinth to keep their minds focused on Christ: "We do not war according to the flesh. For the weapons of our warfare are not carnal but mighty in God for pulling down strongholds, casting down arguments and every high thing that exalts itself against the knowledge of God, bringing every thought into captivity to the obedience of Christ" (2 Cor. 10:3–5).

Paul knew the struggles Christians faced in the world. He was a realist. He knew that in order to survive the

constant barrage of the world's temptations, we would need the strong weapons of the Spirit, our faith, and our obedience. Bringing every thought before God makes obedience possible. God can clearly show us if living out that thought will make us more like Christ. If it won't, we can get rid of it and continue following Him.

I remember interviewing Jim and Sally Conway, a couple who have written a book on mid-life crisis, *Your Marriage Can Survive a Mid-Life Crisis.* Jim had faithfully served as a minister for years, and then he suddenly decided to leave Sally, his children, and his church and go and live in the Caribbean. There was no excitement left in his life. Day had followed predictable day, and he finally felt driven to find himself.

The night before he planned to leave, God asked Jim an intriguing question: "If you trust Me to take care of you if you run away, why don't you trust Me to take care of you if you stay?" Good question, God! Jim thought so too. He stayed with his wife and discovered a new love and a new vitality in serving the Lord. He now describes that phase as a "madness" that came over him, and, looking back, he can hardly believe himself.

It doesn't take much to distract us from walking in obedience and being faithful to our spouses—boredom and a need for excitement, disillusionment with ourselves or someone else, loneliness or pain. We can write Scripture verses on cards and pray through them each day. But we also need friends we can talk honestly with about our thought lives.

I am thankful for the couple of good friends who

know me well enough to ask questions. We have agreed to call one another if we are ever attracted to men other than our husbands. It's easy to make a phone call about a fleeting attraction; it's much harder to bring the attraction into captivity when we harbor it and allow it to develop.

Our agreement may sound strange to you, but it's a great comfort and security to me. I don't go around falling in love with people all the time—I'm very much in love with Norman. But I'm not so naive as to believe that I am above temptation.

We also need to talk openly with our spouses, always communicating our willingness to change and to help meet their needs, as well as communicating our desires and needs. Norman and I have started a new tradition. Once a month we sit down and ask one another, "What can I do to be a better spouse?" We rarely deal with major issues—little things seem to matter the most. I've asked Norman to say good-bye when he's finished talking with me on the phone. He usually just hangs up and it drives me nuts. Norman has asked me to stop commenting on his driving at fifty-yard intervals!

We are in our marriage for the rest of our lives so it makes sense that we would make it the best it could be. Paul didn't mean for us to stifle our imaginations when he said "take every thought into captivity." Rather he meant that we should keep our thoughts on God so we would not wander from the truth. We can lie in bed and imagine ourselves on a beach with Mel Gibson or Michelle Pfieffer, or we can use our fertile imaginations to think of some fun things to do with the one we love.

We will find mercy and forgiveness if we fail in our marriages. But we can bring joy to God's heart by investing in our marriages now. We will also have fun along the way and become encouragements to others rather than warning statistics.

Faithful 'til the End

> Be anxious for nothing, but in everything by
> prayer and supplication, with thanksgiving, let
> your requests be made known to God.
> Philippians 4:6

I have very few heroes. I'm not cynical about people, but I am fairly realistic. We believers are merely frail human beings, doing our best with the grace of God to be more like Jesus. I do have one or two heroes, though—my mother being one and Ruth Bell Graham, another.

You don't get to see very much of the elegant, gifted lady who has stood behind Billy Graham for years. Ruth once said if she became too recognizable, she would dye her hair and move to Europe! At crusades she prefers to sit among the crowds of people—not on the platform—as her beloved husband brings the only message of hope for a hurting world.

Ruth is gifted in her use of words and has a wonderful sense of humor. A talk show host once asked her if in all her years of marriage she had ever considered divorce. "Divorce never," she quipped, "murder often!" One of

my favorite poets, she often expresses my exact feelings through her carefully penned words.

If I were allowed one word to describe Ruth Bell Graham, I would choose *faithful*. There must have been days when it was difficult to be the wife of such a well-known man, times when it would have been good to have him home to help in a family crisis or to share a special sunset.

Recently, I spent some time with Ruth in the Grahams' lovely mountain home in North Carolina. Mementos of years of faithful service to Christ across the globe and in her home surround her there. Pictures of her children, grandchildren, and great-grandchildren adorn every tabletop. She's the mother of five, grandmother of nineteen, and great-grandmother of three.

I asked Ruth how she handled the tough days as a young wife and mother. How did she respond when she was, at times, pushed into an unsolicited spotlight? Her answer was simple yet profound.

"Worship and worry cannot exist at the same time in the same heart," she said. "They are mutually exclusive."

Ruth then told me about a time when she awoke in the middle of the night, concerned about one of her children. Unable to sleep, she got out of bed, picked up her Bible, and began to read: "Be anxious for nothing, but in everything by prayer and supplication, with thanksgiving, let your requests be made known to God" (Phil. 4:6).

Ruth realized that the missing ingredient in her heart at that time was thanksgiving, so she began to thank God for this son, for his life, for the joy he had brought

to their home. Her burden lifted, and she fell back asleep.

We can pray and make our requests known to God. But we have to trust that God will answer our prayers. Thanksgiving helps us do that. When we pray with thanksgiving, we are saying we believe He will answer us and provide for our needs or for the needs of those we love—and we will be happy with His provision.

Offering thanks helps us release control, acknowledge God's strength, and rejoice that He can take care of what we have brought before Him. It frees us from our worries and allows us to rest.

I am thankful for that night with Ruth Graham. We continued to talk after she told me her story until it was time to turn in for the night. Ruth made me some hot tea, which I took to my room. After I had crawled in bed, a little picture on the wall caught my eye. It said, "Edge your days with prayer; they are less likely to unravel." I knew that was how this faithful woman lived.

Mercy for Rambo

"I cried out to the LORD
because of my
affliction,
And He answered me."
Jonah 2:2

$\mathcal{T}$ he horror and shame of Vietnam still disturbs us like an annoying fly in the summer's heat. So many healthy men and women came back from that war ravaged—unable to return to "business as usual," for business as usual seemed ridiculous after the madness they had experienced. Many others went to Vietnam as ticking time bombs, just waiting to explode. Dr. Mickey Block, Special Forces Commando, was one such person.

Mickey spent his childhood being moved from orphanages to foster homes. He had been taken out of an abusive home, his body covered in cigarette burns, and experienced the trauma of being separated from his brothers and sisters. He continued to experience abuse as he moved from home to home. His anger built, his rage

grew and festered, and then he hit the killing fields of Vietnam.

Mickey's life in Vietnam was drinking, killing, and whorehouses. Being sober meant facing the reality of war—seeing your best buddy killed in front of you or carrying the tiny charred body of a six-month-old baby to a medical hospital. It was a reality most wanted to escape rather than endure.

Mickey's patience with anyone talking about love in the middle of this horror quickly wore away. So he nearly went crazy when he met a man in his unit named Dave Roever. Dave was a Christian man and talked incessantly about a loving God. Sometimes Mickey could hear Dave whispering prayers after lights out.

Mickey flaunted his habits, hoping to annoy the "preacher man." While Dave would sit on his bunk, playing his guitar and singing at night, Mickey would sit on his bunk, finishing off a case of beer.

Eight months after Dave and Mickey had been in Vietnam, a grenade exploded in the preacher man's face. Dave was transferred out of Mickey's unit, and Mickey assumed that Dave was silenced forever.

Mickey met with a similar fate one rainy evening after that. He and his company were on patrol in a free-fire zone—complete enemy territory. A young, inexperienced American crew came up behind Mickey's boat and, in the blinding rain, assumed they had come in contact with the enemy. They opened up with eight machine guns on Mickey's boat. "It was like standing in a pitch dark room and having hundreds of people shoot-

ing off flashbulbs in your face," Mickey said in an interview.

The bullets ripped into Mickey's body, lifting him up and throwing him to the ground. He lay there, cold and bleeding. He knew he was dying. He could hear people around him, crying and telling God they were sorry for the way they had lived. Sounds of choppers, coming to take out the wounded, echoed in the distance.

As Mickey lay in the darkness, he had a vision of Jesus hanging on the cross. Next to Jesus, another man hung, dying. Mickey could remember from Sunday school the story of the thief on the cross who deserved to go to hell. Jesus had helped that man, but Mickey felt he couldn't ask for the same help. He had lived too wretchedly. Despite his feelings, Mickey asked God to hear his life's confession. Then, everything went black.

During the next ten years, Mickey underwent thirty-three operations. His right leg was amputed above the knee, and the skin from his chest was grafted to his left hand.

Mickey married and had two beautiful children. He had become addicted to drugs and alcohol which almost ruined his marriage. He determined to take his own life but didn't want his children to suffer the grief of such a loss. He was alone in a living hell and desperate.

Mickey cried out to God for help but couldn't seem to reach Him. As he pondered this plight, he turned on the radio and began to listen as a Vietnam veteran talked about having lost forty percent of his flesh to a grenade. Mickey sat up, startled.

This was the voice of the "preacher man"! And he was still talking about the love of God.

Thirteen years after they had last seen each other, Mickey and Dave were reunited. That day, Mickey discovered the mercy of God and yielded his life to Christ.

Mickey was like Jonah as he cried out to God because of his affliction. Jonah had run from the direction God wanted him to go, but he ran right into the belly of a fish. From the depths, "cast out" from God's sight, Jonah turned to God's "holy temple" and he found God's mercy:

> Those who regard worthless idols
> Forsake their own Mercy.
> But I will sacrifice to You
> With the voice of thanksgiving;
> I will pay what I have vowed.
> Salvation is of the LORD (Jonah
>   2:8–9).

Although he had run far from God, Jonah knew God was his mercy. He returned to God and found life and salvation in Him. Thus he was able to offer thanks to God.

I'll never understand why so many people have to experience hell before they ever taste heaven. But no matter how far you've walked away from God, when you finally cry out to Him, He can reach out and bring you back home.

The Heavenly Lottery

Then Jesus said to those Jews who believed Him,
"If you abide in My word, you are My disciples
indeed. And you shall know the truth, and the
truth shall make you free."
John 8:31, 32

I watched a four-hour movie on the life of Jim Jones
one evening and found myself intrigued by this disturbed man. A few days later I discovered that the guest
on my daily talk show, "Heart to Heart," had known Jim
Jones very well. His name was Hue Fortsan, a member
of the People's Church and Mrs. Jones's personal body-
guard. He was one of only three who escaped the poi-
soned Kool-Aid® episode in Guyana.

As I sat and listened to this man, who has now found a
deep personal relationship with Christ, I was amazed
that such a man could be drawn in by Jim Jones. But as
he began to tell his story, it became a little clearer. He
described Jim as an electric speaker. Whenever Jim stood
up to speak, people were pulled in by the passion of his
words and the fire that burned in his eyes. He was a lov-

ing man who welcomed all and, for the lonely and the disillusioned, he became a savior. As he built his empire and extended his influence over the lives of those in the church, he became more real to them than Jesus was. Jim was touchable; he was there in the flesh. Hue said, "When a new issue arose that troubled many, such as when Jim said it was okay for him to sleep with many women other than his wife, he was so forceful, so charismatic and believable that everyone backed down."

I am sure that if we had sat around a dinner table with members of the People's Church five years before the tragedy and laid it out for them, not one would have believed that such a thing was possible. But deception is a slippery slope and we can find ourselves miles away from the plumb line of God's truth before we ever realize we have moved. We are told that the truth will set us free, but we also know that lies from the sweetest mouth can imprison a willing heart.

I don't mean to suggest that I see another Guyana tragedy brewing, but I am troubled by tempting deceptions that hang in the air, like the idea God wants us all to be healthy, wealthy, and wise. Surely people would line the streets for hours to get a ticket for a religion like that. But God's not a giant slot machine in the sky. He asks for our undivided attention and He alone decides which path each one of us must walk.

The secret to not being taken prisoner is found in John 8:31—"abiding" in God's word. In the eighth chapter of John, Jesus presents Himself and God, His Father, as true, and He tells the group of Jewish people listening what truth will do for them. God's word is truth, and that truth makes us free. As long as we live the words Jesus spoke, as long as we live the life He, the final Word, lived, we will be abiding in God's word and we will be free.

When Jesus told a group of Jewish people that living in His word could set them free, they began to question Him. How could He make them free? They thought their heritage made them free. What could Jesus do for them?

Jesus responded, "Whoever commits sin is a slave of sin. . . . If the Son makes you free, you shall be free indeed" (John 8:34, 36). Jesus is our freedom; Jesus is true. There is no other place where we can find freedom from slavery to sin or deception. Our heritage doesn't free us from sin. Gaining wealth or prosperity doesn't cleanse our souls or give us a relationship with Christ.

Jesus describes His disciples as sheep and says, "My sheep hear My voice, and I know them . . . And I give them eternal life, and they shall never perish; neither shall anyone snatch them out of My hand" (John 10:27–28). If we believe and live Christ's truth, we can be secure that we will not be led astray by empty deception or people who appear to be Christlike.

We need strong people around us to help us remain committed to the truth. Perhaps if Jim Jones had been surrounded by strong men and women who loved God and loved him, that horror could have been avoided. But today we have the opportunity to walk away from lies, to study God's word and "hide it" in our hearts so that

we don't sin against God (Ps. 119:11). There will be many things that sound good, but aren't necessarily true. Just ask the emperor what he now thinks about his new clothes!

Shining the Light at Home

"Let your light so shine before men, that they may see your good works and glorify your Father in heaven. . . . Take heed that you do not do your charitable deeds before men, to be seen by them."
Matthew 5:16; 6:1

*T*he best role models are those people who are part of our everyday lives—our parents, our spouses, our neighbors—not people we see on television. When Dale Hanson Bourke interviewed me for *Religious Broadcasting* magazine, we discussed Christian broadcasting's move away from being personality driven. I've been happy for this change.

Pastors, evangelists, Christian musicians—all of us who have larger-than-life personae are still better role models to the people who see us at home and in our neighborhood than we are to the public who sees us only on TV. The greatest endorsements we have come not from other famous people who may interview us or write our biographies, but from the people we've lived with every day.

Each year, between Thanksgiving and Christmas, several of my closest friends and I tour twelve to fourteen cities, performing the "Young Messiah," a contemporary musical version of Handel's classical work. I've enjoyed making new friends on this tour, one of whom is Larnelle Harris.

The first time I heard Larnelle sing, I was left breathless. His voice is an exquisitely honed instrument he can use in almost any way. Larnelle has also impressed me as a role model, however, as I've come to know his family and church friends. His wife, Mitsy, will tell you he's a great husband. His children say he's a wonderful father. And his church friends report what a fine deacon he is.

The apostle Paul also seemed to think a person's reputation at home was as important as—or more so than—his reputation in the community or on stage. He instructed Timothy to choose leaders for the church, role models for the church, based on their reputations not only in the community but also in their households: "If a man does not know how to rule his own house, how will he take care of the church of God? . . . Moreover he must have a good testimony among those who are outside, lest he fall into reproach" (1 Tim. 3:5, 7).

If we aren't good role models at home, chances are we won't be effective role models in public or on stage. We can put our best faces forward and perhaps convince people for a while of our strength or perfection. But our shells will crack sometime and the emptiness will be exposed.

Larnelle has established a good reputation at home and in the community by choosing to love and serve his family first and by choosing to make himself accountable to a local body of believers. This renowned artist has often passed up great opportunities to be present at large, well-paying events because he wants to watch his children grow up. "My kids won't remember if I played to twenty thousand people on Thanksgiving," he has said, "but they will remember if I am home."

His church family supports him as he grows in his relationship with the Lord. They gives thanks to God as Larnelle changes and matures. And if he is tempted to wander, they are there to bring him back. As with all of us, accountability gives him the chance to develop a lifestyle consistent with what he says he believes.

It may seem Jesus' admonition to let our "light so shine before men" would be more effectively carried out were we to shine before thousands. But thousands can't see the way we live each day. Thousands don't know how we respond when we stub our toe or when dinner burns or when the children come in late. Thousands don't see how willing we are to shine at home. And thousands won't be deeply changed by our light that shines down from the stage. The few will be changed by our light, however.

I am inspired for a moment by a personality who comes into my life and offers a dramatic challenge. But I am changed by those I live with day in and day out. They are the people whose light illumines my path and causes me to be grateful to God.

Held Above the Waters

When you pass through the waters,
I will be with you;
And through the rivers,
They shall not overflow you.
Isaiah 43:2

*E*lectricity filled the air in the hospital waiting room in Fayetteville, Georgia. Ike Reighard and his wife, Cindy, were waiting for the arrival of their first child. At home the baby's room was ready. A music box waited to coax a reluctant child to sleep with a sweet tune. Teddy bears and rabbits sat "toy-store new," ready to be loved and to lose their ears.

Ike pastored a large church and so the waiting room at the hospital was filled with friends and family who wanted to share in the joy of this gift of life. In the labor and delivery room, Ike sat by Cindy's side, squeezing her hand and savoring the last few moments of being "just the two of them." Around Cindy's neck lay a diamond snowflake necklace that Ike bought as a gift for his beloved wife. The light reflecting from the diamond caught Ike's eye and he was warmed by the memory of the gift. Life seemed complete.

When Cindy knew her time was near, she urged Ike to pop down to the waiting room and tell her parents. He fulfilled his mission and was only steps away from Cindy's door when the doctor rushed out and grabbed his shoulders. "Mr. Reighard, we can save Cindy or your baby, but not both. Something has gone very wrong."

"My wife!" Ike choked. "Save my wife." He fell against the wall as the medical emergency team raced by. A few moments later, the doctor returned. They were both gone—Ike's precious wife and his little one were dead.

That night Ike returned to his home alone. The rabbits and teddy bears mocked him from their corner; the music box remained closed.

The next few days passed with Ike in numb disbelief, but then reality set in. Everyone else returned to their daily routines, and Ike was left with a lonely, empty house. He thought of all the words of comfort he had used as a pastor to give hope to others, but they were empty for him. He was angry; he was sad and so depressed he could hardly get up in the morning.

One day Ike pulled out a drawer and came across a little box of Cindy's things from the hospital. He opened the box and saw the diamond snowflake. The chain was broken where the doctors had pulled it off her neck when they tried to save her life. Ike held the pendant up to the sunlight, but it wouldn't shine. Cindy had always commented on its sparkle, but now it was dull and lifeless. A few days later Ike took the necklace to a jeweler

and asked him to clean it and see if the luster could be restored. The jeweler worked on it for a while and then told Ike that it no longer reflected the light because the diamonds had been covered by a layer of dried blood.

Ike stumbled to the car and wept. He wept because he missed Cindy. He wept for the child he never knew. But he also wept because he knew he was not alone. The blood reminded him of Christ's death on the cross, and he finally understood that Jesus knew God was with Him, even in His darkest moments. Ike knew God was with him too.

God promises to be with us, never to leave the ones He loves. Isaiah 43:1–2 says,

> "Fear not, for I have redeemed you;
> I have called you by your name;
> You are Mine.
> When you pass through the
>   waters, I will be with you."

We don't have to fear walking through the waters of pain and sorrow. God will not leave us alone.

God proclaims to the Israelites in this passage of Scripture that He is their creator and their Lord and Savior. God reminds them of the times throughout history He has rescued them from trouble since they are "precious" in His sight. These words apply to us today as well. God created us for His "glory" (v. 7). God will not reject or desert His own creation, the ones who will someday "declare [His] praise" (v. 21). Our redeemer

loves us and will bring us through the waters so we can one day declare His praise.

> "Therefore you are My witnesses,"
> Says the LORD, "that I am God.
> Indeed before the day was, I am He;
> And there is no one who can
>   deliver out of My hand;
> I work, and who will reverse it?"
>   (Isa. 43:12–13).

God has all power and no one can stand against Him. Nothing can stop His love for us, and nothing can keep Him from being with us—"no one . . . can deliver out of [His] hand." No one could keep God from Christ, and no one could keep Christ from going to the Cross for us. We can be confident that even in our deepest sorrow, we are held up by the one with the nail-pierced hands.

Peace in the Fast Lane

"In returning and rest you shall be saved;
In quietness and confidence shall be
    your strength."
Isaiah 30:15

*S*tress is a hot topic these days. Books discuss it.
Seminar speakers dissect and analyze it. Mega-vitamins
absorb it.

The Minirth-Meier Clinic offered a session on stress
management for the employees at CBN. I intended to go
as I have great respect for these doctors, but I was too
stressed out to make it!

One of my friends from England experienced shopping stress on her first visit to the States. After recovering from chemotherapy, she and her husband felt a
change of scenery would do her good, so they decided to
come to America.

One day he parked outside of a large supermarket
while she went inside to pick up something for their evening meal. Twenty minutes later, she rushed out of the
store, empty-handed, tears streaming down her cheeks.

The variety of choices in the store overwhelmed her so she was unable to shop.

I, too, have days when I have so many things to do I get nothing done—the whole scenario is too much to bear.

Traditionally, women deal more effectively with stress because society allows us to cry. Tears are a safety valve to diffuse emotions that overload us. Sometimes our emotions are triggered by the most unlikely events.

A few weeks ago, I felt totally "maxed out." I was working my regular five days a week at the "700 Club," continuing my concert schedule on weekends, beginning to write this book, and completing the recording for a new album. Doing all of that while still trying to run my home and be a good wife had stretched me more than I realized.

I broke away from the pressure by taking Charlie, my West Highland white terrier, out for a quick walk at lunchtime. We live in a quiet neighborhood, so I felt comfortable taking off his leash to let him explore. Before I realized what was happening, Charlie ran off the sidewalk and slid down a storm drain under the walk.

I fell to my knees above the drain and called Charlie's name. He barked twice in response and then was silent.

I raced back to the house and called the animal rescue service. The people at the office told me to stay with him and keep talking to him—it would take twenty minutes for them to get to my neighborhood. I grabbed a flashlight and ran back to the spot where Charlie had fallen.

Shining the light through a hole in the metal plate, I could see the muddy ledge about five feet below me,

where Charlie was standing. If he slipped off that ledge and fell further down, I would lose him.

Twenty minutes would be too long to wait for the rescue service, I decided. So I ran from door to door, throughout the neighborhood, looking for someone to help lift the metal plate. Eventually, I found a neighbor who was home, and with the aid of two crowbars, we lifted the grid and got Charlie out.

My little white dog was now black with dirt. So I took him home and gave him a bath. He then ran off into the yard as happy as could be, and I sat down on the floor and cried for thirty minutes. When Norman came home and saw me in tears, he thought my mother had died or I'd been diagnosed with some malignant disease!

The fear of this escapade would have upset me on a good day when I felt rested and fresh. But my prolonged crying that day was caused by the stress of my work that week.

An article in *Newsweek* said that stress in the workplace costs the U.S. economy $150 billion annually.★ Emotional traumas from stress can lead to depression or nervous breakdowns. And prolonged stress causes high blood pressure, heart disease, asthma, diabetes, and other physical ailments.

Christians experiencing depression from stress often also experience guilt. We feel we should be able to cope and "do all things through Christ who strengthens me." We move homes or change jobs; we face marriage or di-

---

★*Newsweek,* April 25, 1988, 28–33.

vorce or death; a woman bears a child and becomes a working mother. We experience change at a rapid pace; yet, we don't always realize how the changes affect us, the pressure these changes create. And when we are struggling to "triumph," the enemy loves to disturb our sense of balance and whisper "fraud" in our ears, causing us to try harder to live in our own strength.

Isaiah told the nation Israel that they would find strength in quietness and confidence, that God would rescue them when they turned to Him. The prophet promised Israel that God would be gracious to them if they repented from their rebellion and returned to Him; in fact, Isaiah said, God was waiting to be gracious to them (30:18). At the sound of Israel's cry, God would answer them and they would not cry anymore (v. 19). The people would not listen to this prophecy until they experienced destruction, however. Instead, they would persist in seeing themselves riding into battle on swift horses, anticipating victory.

We can apply the principle of Isaiah's prophecy to ourselves when we are demanding too much of ourselves. God has marvelously designed our bodies to warn us when we've had too much. When we ignore these warning signs and continue to push ourselves to do more and be more, we are persisting in the belief that we are indestructible. We are living as if our strength is limitless. Eventually, we will be like the Israelites, who trusted in their own strength rather than turn to God. We will be "as a pole on top of a mountain"—alone, defeated, broken.

We need to find time for a little fun. Perhaps you are

like me and reason that you don't have time for fun. But the truth is we can't afford not to take time to rest and to turn to God.

I am learning to have a little "me" time every day. Some days I sit in the garden and listen to the birds and watch Charlie annoy the squirrels. Some days I sneak off in the afternoon and see a movie. Some days I close my eyes for thirty minutes and take a siesta. Most of all, I take time to remind myself of the unfailing love of God. When you take time daily to remember that God is still on the throne and your name is etched on His palm, you can face each day knowing that He asks you to do only what He gives you the strength to do. So let the telephone ring!

Never Say Never

"Then I will sow her for Myself in the earth,
  And I will have mercy on her who had not
    obtained mercy;
  Then I will say to those who were not My
    people,
 'You are My people!'
  And they shall say, 'You are my God!'"
Hosea 2:23

*R*oy and Pauline Harthern were raised in a godly
tradition in England. They met there and married in the
States. As Roy and Pauline grew together through the
years, they watched marriages around them, even those
of Christian leaders, fall apart. Yet, they knew theirs
would never do the same—they were safe.

Roy accepted the pastorate at Calvary Assembly in
Orlando, Florida, and led the church to new growth.
When he first joined the staff, there were two hundred
and seventy members. Under Roy's pastoral care and
that of his staff, the church grew to more than seven
thousand members.

A woman in the church came to Roy for counsel one day, and eventually, after several months, they fell in love. When the elders confronted Roy with his sin, he knew he would have to tell Pauline. He was convinced she would kill herself. Instead, when he told her about his affair and that it was all over, Pauline was "magnificent" and Roy fell apart.

For weeks, Roy cried as he faced the consequences of his actions, losing his job and his church. But he finally regained hope and began to smile again. He felt as if he did have a future.

As Roy improved, something in Pauline snapped. In her experience as a minister's daughter and then as a minister's wife, she had never been allowed to vent anger. When she learned of Roy's betrayal, she denied her anger and wasn't able to receive God's healing for her pain. So when Roy was ready to live again, Pauline was just breaking. It was one thing to watch Roy broken and crushed by his actions, but to hear him laugh again was more than she could bear.

Betrayal can break us more easily than other tragedies. We wonder if we can ever regain trust for the other person—what if it were to happen again?

Pauline felt vulnerable and naked before Christ. Her bruises were deep and needed time to heal. She found, however, that God gives us time—time to weep, time to be angry, time to heal. And Roy gave her time too.

The Old Testament talks about a divine romance between God and Israel:

"I will betroth you to Me forever;
  Yes, I will betroth you to Me
  In righteousness and justice,
  In lovingkindness and mercy;
  I will betroth you to Me in faithfulness"
    (Hosea 2:19–20).

God's relationship to Israel is likened to that of a husband to his wife. God claims Israel as His bride. He proclaims His love for her: "I will betroth you to Me. . . . In lovingkindness and mercy." He proclaims His faithfulness: "I will betroth you to Me forever." Perhaps the most beautiful part of the romance is that God remains unchanging, faithful, in this marriage, whether Israel is faithful or not.

The book of Hosea vividly portrays God's response to an unfaithful Israel. God calls Hosea to marry an adulterous woman and uses this relationship to mirror to Israel their unfaithfulness. God does not ignore His bride's behavior. He does not hide His pain. But neither does He stop loving Israel. He never disowns her. Instead, He says:

"I will have mercy on her who had not obtained
  mercy;
 Then I will say to those who were not My people,
'You are My people!'
 And they shall say, 'You are my God!' " (Hosea 2:23).

God tells His bride to come back. He offers His mercy and forgiveness.

This passage portrays a joyful reunion between a grace-giving husband and a thankful, repentant wife. The adulterous wife has not earned the mercy she receives. But when she returns to God and sees He still claims her, she shouts out her thanks through her renewed commitment to Him—"You are my God!" Ironically, this picture of grace is given to us in the Old Testament, where people were judged on how well they kept the rules and obeyed the Law. God does not offer a plan for Israel to work her way back to Him—He does not insist she prove herself to Him. Instead, He offers His mercy.

God understands the pain a spouse bears when his or her mate commits adultery. He is able to respond perfectly to unfaithfulness; we are not. But if we choose to turn to God, He can heal our pain and give us the ability to offer His grace and forgiveness to a mate's unfaithfulness. He heals the wounds of the faithful spouse; He heals the shame of the adulterous spouse.

Today Roy and Pauline have mended hearts, but their healing involved risk. Pauline had to choose to love Roy again, and God gave her the grace to do this. Roy had to let Pauline be angry with him—and God healed his shame. They both had to learn that to love means to abandon self and to offer forgiveness. In the process, they learned about the divine romance God desires to have with us—"A Fine Romance" I've called it in one of my lyrics. It is a relationship founded in grace and mercy and kindness rather than a religion or code of rules whereby we must prove ourselves and our trustworthiness.

A Fine Romance

When I was just a child
I saw that love can strip you bare
Can take a bright and hopeful heart
And in a moment tear your world apart.
No warning bells or neon signs
Prepare you for the pain
Of having loved
And having lost
And can we love again?

It seemed so cold and futile
To step outside the door,
To watch our candles flame within
Proud, but helpless in the changing wind.
We live to feel the air beneath
Our battered, broken wings
For having flown
And having known
A taste of better things.

A fine romance
Oh, do we dare
To take a second chance
When God the Father
Asked me for a dance
He set His heart upon a fine romance.

And all my life, I've been afraid
Of letting people in
Of giving them the power to wound,

To take my ship and watch it run aground.
So help me, Lord,
Unclench my fists
Throw open shuttered doors
And in this dance
This fine romance
The fragrance will be Yours.

Room for One More

The LORD builds up Jerusalem;
He gathers together the outcasts of Israel.
He heals the brokenhearted
And binds up their wounds.
Psalm 147:2–3

*J*erry and Sandy Tucker were told they couldn't have any children. Today they have thirty!

The Tuckers are the founders and directors of the Galilean home in Kentucky that cares for physically, mentally, and emotionally handicapped children. They travel to Haiti, Honduras, Guatemala, Afghanistan, and Brazil, and bring handicapped children to their Christian home for medical treatment. After recovery and nurture, the children either return to their homes or are adopted into the ample bosom of the Tuckers' household. It's quite a sight to see the outside of their home—thirty-two pairs of shoes lined up on the porch!

Jerry and Sandy never stopped to debate "If God is good, why is there suffering?" amidst the disappointment of their not being able to have children. Instead,

125

they understood suffering to be part of a fallen world. They trusted that God was their loving Father, and they chose to follow Him by loving the unwanted of the world.

It's hard to be faithful to God when you're suffering, because He often seems to be the One who is withholding the good you want or believe you need. (This is especially true if you have been taught God does not allow bad things to happen.) We can only cling to the truth of the Scriptures. The Bible does not promise that God won't allow suffering in the world. It does show that God provides amidst pain.

David praises God in the Psalms because he has seen Him "gather together the outcasts" and "heal" and "bind the wounds" of the brokenhearted. He doesn't say, "Praise God for keeping us from being brokenhearted." Or "Thank God, no one is alone anymore." Instead, David thanks God that in His mighty power and infinite understanding, He "lifts up the humble." God provides for the broken in ways we cannot anticipate. We can't guess what God will do, and His plan certainly may not look like what we would have imagined Him to do. (Who would have imagined the day the doctor delivered the news of their barrenness that someday this couple would be the adoptive parents of thirty children and the foster parents of more than two hundred?)

God "does not delight in the strength of the horse; / He takes no pleasure in the legs of a man," says David. "The LORD takes pleasure in those who fear Him, / In those who hope in His mercy" (Ps. 147:10–11). God wants us to trust Him, to believe He is merciful despite the "bad things" that happen. And He provides for us when we see our need and are ready to depend on Him.

God "lifted up" Jerry and Sandy Tucker and gave them a love that lifts up the unlovely, the castaways. He helps them love those who have every reason to wonder if there is a God and if He is good. Jerry and Sandy have remembered Jesus' words, "And whoever receives one little child like this in My name receives Me" (Matt. 18:5). So they tell each child who comes into their home about the God who will bind their wounds and heal their hearts with the love of His Son, Jesus.

When Elanue came to the Galilean home from Haiti four years ago, she had one leg and could only hop and crawl. Now, with the help of a prosthetic leg, Elanue has learned to walk. She has also learned from Jerry and Sandy about the greatest healing there is—the healing of forgiveness. When this young woman returned to Haiti, she shared the love and forgiveness of Christ with her family. Today all of her family loves and serves Christ.

Many of the other children have left the Galilean home and become missionaries, sharing the unconditional love the Tuckers shared with them. Like the Tuckers, they have come to believe in God's mercy, and now they are reaching out to offer God's healing to others.

When Hope Refused to Die

> And not only that, but we also glory in tribulations, knowing that tribulation produces perseverance; and perseverance, character; and character, hope.
> Romans 5:3–4

*J*immy Ritter played football throughout his high school years and, as a senior, was named captain of the team. Through the influence of his grandmother, Jimmy had given his life to Christ when he was nine years old. Although his parents were not Christians, Jimmy's grandmother was, and she made sure that he and his brothers went to church.

During the summer months, Jimmy worked for his father, who ran a logging business. One warm day during lunchtime, Jimmy crawled into the grapple of a logging machine to get out of the sun and to catch up on his sleep. Not realizing where Jimmy was, his father went to the machine and started the engine. Anguished cries pierced the air, stopping Ritter cold. He turned off the engine and ran to his son's rescue.

Mr. Ritter rushed his son to the hospital. The doctors announced that his third, fourth, and fifth cervical vertebrae had been crushed, and they gave him a five percent chance of living.

Jimmy lived, though he remained in intensive care for nine weeks. He was then moved as a quadriplegic to an orthopedic hospital. Jimmy clung to his faith, believing there had to be a purpose in all of his suffering.

Jimmy felt the most painful effects of the accident when he finally returned home. He watched his father retreat from him and from the rest of the world. Not knowing what to say, his father avoided him completely. And for two years, his father stayed home from work, unable to face the world.

Because no one at home shared Jimmy's faith, he sought to have fellowship with brothers and sisters in the Christian community. But there, he met with discouragement. People would pray for him and then try to pull him out of his wheelchair. When he still could not move, people accused him of being faithless and sinful.

I'm sure you recoil, as I do, from this kind of Christian barbarism, yet Jimmy's hope remained intact. "Sheila," he told me, "I know without a shadow of a doubt that God can heal me. But let me tell you this—if He does, you won't need to pull me out of my wheelchair; I'll be running!"

Jimmy persevered through the many frustrating days when he felt like throwing in the towel. He is a living example of how tribulations can produce character. Through his tribulations, he has held on to his belief in the goodness of God rather than long to trust in strength

or looks or talent. As he has persevered, he has developed character that reflects God's goodness. He has chosen to love and understand those who make insensitive comments to him. He has loved his father, whose guilt and pain caused him to reject his son.

The loving, selfless, forgiving character chiseled into Jimmy's heart allows him to be filled with hope—hope in something far greater than in God's healing powers. Jimmy's hope is that the love of Christ Jesus can overcome all pain and tribulation.

Tribulations can tear from us the strength or the people or the things we typically trust or place our hope in. We then have two options: to turn to ourselves or to turn to God. When we turn to ourselves, we become bitter or despairing. But when we turn to God, we find that God pours out His love into our hearts by the Holy Spirit. And, Paul says in Romans 5, God's love will not disappoint us.

God's love gives us hope—hope that we have worth apart from what we have or look like or achieve and hope that we will have an everlasting life without pain. Paul does not ask in Romans 5:3–4 that we be excited about the pain we must sometimes endure, but rather that we be excited about the hope and character pain can produce.

Jimmy now has a loving wife and is a man of godly character. He is still in that chair; his body has been crushed. But his hope is alive and well.

Beyond the Barricade

But He was wounded for our transgressions,
He was bruised for our iniquities;
The chastisement for our peace was upon Him,
And by His stripes we are healed.
Isaiah 53:5

*I*t was 3:00 A.M. I sat up in bed, sweat pouring down my back. Where was I?

I was having a nightmare. I had dreamt that someone falsely accused me of murdering another person. No one would believe I was innocent, and I was being taken to the electric chair. When I realized I was awake and not on my way to be electrocuted, I was relieved. A few weeks later, I met a man who had lived my nightmare.

One evening, Harold Morris, a nice, middle-aged American family man, was sitting alone at a bar when two strangers sat down with him. The three men spent a pleasant hour together, talking and drinking, and then Harold left for home. The two men departed shortly after Harold and went to rob a grocery store, shooting and killing a customer.

The men later identified Harold and his car to the police and said they had seen Harold running from the scene of the crime. Morris was arrested and the men testified against him in court. Morris was given two life sentences.

Disbelief and bitterness filled Harold Morris. He planned to get revenge on the men by having them killed. Just before two prisoners were to be released from prison, Harold gave them his life's savings to murder the two men who had sent him to prison. The prisoners took his money and used it to give themselves a new start after they were released.

Ashamed of his fate, Morris wouldn't tell his family he was in prison. His first five years there, he didn't receive a letter or a visitor. Living with what he described as the "scum of the earth" hardened his heart. At times his inner rage would spill over into violence and he would end up in "the hole," a solitary confinement blackout cell.

A fellow prisoner gave Morris an old battered Bible one day and he began to read in Isaiah 53:

He was wounded for our transgressions,
He was bruised for our iniquities;
The chastisement for our peace was upon Him.
And by His stripes we are healed.

Here was someone who could identify with Harold. The passage was about Jesus, an innocent man who was punished and tortured for a crime He never committed. In Jesus, Harold found someone who understood his broken heart. Harold discovered a difference in Jesus' story, however. Jesus was led like a lamb to the slaughter, Harold read. "And as a sheep before its shearers is silent, / So He opened not his mouth" (Isa. 53:7). Harold had tried but had not been able to defend himself against his accusers. This Jesus *chose* not to defend himself against His accusers. That was a miracle!

Recalling his years of anger and planning revenge, Harold began to understand the crimes he had committed—his crimes against God. In the filth of his cell, Harold asked Jesus to help him. He asked Jesus to forgive him and to take away his hatred.

Finally, after serving nine and a half years for a crime he never committed, Harold was paroled. He enrolled in Bible school and began to learn more about Jesus. And he forgave those who had wronged him.

Today, Harold Morris travels across the country, speaking to teenagers in high schools about the choices they make in their lives. He tells his story with such passion that hundreds of lives have been changed.

People whose life stories are as dramatic as Harold's often give Christ everything they have in service. They seem to know that life is in Jesus. With Him, there is life and the assurance of heaven. Without Him, there is death and the certainty of hell.

When I woke from my nightmare that morning I thought for a while of those who cannot snap out of the end of their life as if they were snapping out of a bad dream. It made me bolder about sharing the love of God with others.

Footwashing 101

"If I then, your Lord and Teacher, have washed
your feet, you also ought to wash one another's
feet."
John 13:14

I rushed onto the waiting plane and fell into my seat.
The young woman in the seat next to me seemed pleasant enough, but she obviously wanted to talk. And I was
busy.

I made it clear I didn't have time to chat because I had
so much work to do. I pulled my briefcase from under
my seat, shuffled through a stack of papers, and settled
back with a pen in hand.

Do you know what I was doing? I was preparing to
minister that night to a group of Christians who probably already knew everything I had to say. But I felt my
time was more precious than the time of the woman next
to me because I had a "ministry."

I don't believe any of us *has* a ministry. We *are* ministries. When we are involved in ministries, however, we
can easily become part of the "ministry" circus—the

134

thinking that God's hand is on our lives so we are excused from accountability or acts of kindness and mercy and other godly behavior.

Stuart McAlpine is a busy man who cares for the people of a large church in Washington D.C. After appearing as a guest on the 700 Club one day, he overheard a conversation I was having with a colleague. We were worried about a friend who seemed battered and worn out from heartache. I had invited six of this woman's friends to come to my house that day to meet with her and pray for her and reassure her of our love and commitment. Stuart interrupted our conversation and offered, as a pastor, to come with us. We were surprised, but gladly agreed.

I was moved that afternoon as I watched Stuart sit with our friend and share God's Word and Christ's love with her. He had not hesitated to serve by taking time to be with one wounded person. Stuart McAlpine was as much of a ministry that day he came to the quiet of my home as he was onstage on the 700 Club or in the pulpit in his church.

We become ministries when we lay aside our agendas and enroll in "Footwashing 101." Remember what happened after the disciples had eaten the Last Supper with Christ? Jesus stripped Himself down to His loin cloth, took a bowl and a towel, and washed His friends' feet. Jesus was exhibiting true Christian leadership as He humbled Himself, made Himself an example, and served the disciples.

In his letter to the Philippians, Paul wrote that we ought to become like Jesus, who "made Himself of no

reputation, taking the form of a servant, . . . humbled Himself and became obedient to the point of death" (Phil. 2:7–8). Jesus did not try to protect His reputation or position as the Son of God. Instead, He became like us and, more miraculously, He served us. He didn't discriminate, limiting His associations to the wealthy or nobles or intellectuals. He talked with sinners and women and prostitutes and children—the "outcasts" of the day.

After Jesus finished washing His disciples' feet, He told them, "You call Me Teacher and Lord, and you say well, for so I am. If I then, your Lord and Teacher, have washed your feet, you also ought to wash one another's feet. For I have given you an example, that you should do as I have done to you. Most assuredly, I say to you, a servant is not greater than his master; nor is he who is sent greater than he who sent him" (John 13:13–16). The Teacher gave His students the place of honor before Himself—an example of how we are to live. Now we can honor others before ourselves.

The Lord is kind and gracious to me when He shows me my hypocrisy as He did the day I sat on that plane. He is gentle as He calls me to be real, and He gives me wonderful examples of people like Stuart McAlpine, who are true servants, who esteem others more highly than themselves.

"If you know these things," Jesus told the disciples His last evening with them, "happy are you if you do them" (v. 17). We are most content, not when we receive honor from the ministries we "have," but when we become ministers—servants—to others.

Prodigal, Come Home

"There is hope in your future, says the LORD,
That your children shall come back to their
     own border."
Jeremiah 31:17

I've often thought how hard it must be for Christian parents whose children choose to walk away from their faith. I've watched my friends raise their four lively children as best they knew how, only to see them all turn away from the kingdom. I've listened as this couple has been told to pray for their children, to counsel them or challenge them, but I've never heard the parents told to forgive them.

Quin Sherrer's advice to Christian parents is just that—forgive your wandering children. Quin's three children decided to go their own way, away from the Lord. Quin was almost heartbroken, but God gave her wisdom amidst her despair.

First, she realized as she watched her children that she had created pain for her parents and they had made mistakes as they raised her. She asked her parents' forgive-

137

ness for her offenses against them and forgave them for their offenses against her. The most godly parents are fallible. They need our forgiveness as we do theirs. Then, Quin humbled herself before her children by forgiving them.

Perhaps the greatest hurdle to overcome in offering forgiveness is pride. Parents often fear losing their place of authority and strength in their children's lives. They are offended that their child has disappointed them and made them look bad in front of others. This fear, however, can catapult parents into a power play with children that destroys the children or leaves them feeling resentful forever.

A couple came to talk with me after a concert in Dallas, Texas. They showed me a picture of a beautiful seventeen-year-old girl who had taken her life on her birthday that year. Weeping, the parents told me about the note she had left behind: "Mom and Dad I can't take it anymore. The pressure is too great. It would be better for everyone if I were gone."

Children buckle when they feel as if they are failures in the eyes of their families. So many turn and run away. We all need to know whether we are doing well or poorly. But we all need to feel that, despite our performance, we are loved simply for who we are. This assurance is not always easy to give, but with God's help it is possible. If we can't find this assurance at home, we'll look for it elsewhere.

Quin believes that when parents are humble enough to show mercy and grace—when parents are willing to ask for and to offer forgiveness—their children will be

freed to ask for forgiveness. This willingness is a sign of true authority and strength, not an abdication of it.

What does forgiveness look like? An open door, a willingness to welcome the children home, anytime the children are ready to come. A forgiving parent is one who is farsighted—one who is willing to overlook the offenses of the present in order to preserve a lifetime relationship.

God's forgiveness of the rebelling Israel sets the example for how parents can forgive their own children.

> "Is Ephraim My dear son?
> Is he a pleasant child?
> For though I spoke against him,
> I earnestly remember him still;
> Therefore My heart yearns for him;
> I will surely have mercy on him," says the LORD
> (Jer. 31:20).

God remembers His child, even though He has been angry with him. Even while God is angry, He yearns for His child, so when His son returns, He will have mercy.

Parents are not called to deny their pain or the seriousness or wrongness of a child's offense. God does not hide His fury when Israel (or His children today) rebel against Him:

> "Behold, the whirlwind of the LORD
> Goes forth with fury, . . .
> The fierce anger of the LORD will not return
> . . . until He has performed the intents of His heart"
> (Jer. 30:23–24).

But parents are called to lay aside their anger—to love even while they are angry—in order to be ready to receive the child who is sorry for his or her offense.

God's love is everlasting, says Jeremiah. It promises hope for the future of the prodigal: "Yes, I have loved you with an everlasting love; / Therefore with loving-kindness I have drawn you" (Jer. 31:3). His love for us does not depend on our good behavior. God deals justly with those who turn against Him. But He will never reject the child who repents. Relationships with rebelling children can be restored; children can return home to their families.

Quin and her husband prayed faithfully for years with little result. But they kept on loving, kept on forgiving, kept on praying. Today, all three children are loving and serving God. One is a missionary in Copenhagen; one has been involved in missions work in Germany; and one creates sacred banners as visual worship aids.

Each child took the long road home, but each one knew that at the end of that journey he would be reunited with parents who loved and forgave him. The Sherrer parents are like those in the lyric that follows. They longed for their children's return and represented to their children a God who loves and forgives.

> Did you wonder if you'd gone too far?
> Would you find a welcome just the way you are?
> At the table there's a place with a picture of
> your face
> And we've left the light on just to guide you
> home.

Prodigal, come home
We are waiting for you
Prodigal, come home
How we miss you
For the party can't begin
'Til the family's gathered in
Prodigal, we love you
Don't you know we miss you
Prodigal, come home.

Scars

"I know that you can do everything,
  And that no purpose of Yours can be withheld
    from You."
Job 42:2

I was sitting in my dressing room at nine o'clock one morning when Cheryl Gardener, the producer of "Heart to Heart," came in to talk about that morning's program.

"Sheila, I want you to look at this," Cheryl said, showing me a photograph of a good-looking, tall Washington state trooper. He looked as if he were in his late twenties, early thirties.

"He looks like a nice man," I commented.

"Nice, he is. I just hope you won't be too shocked when you meet him. He doesn't look like this anymore."

When I saw Michael, I was horrified. I couldn't recognize him from the picture.

Michael and I sat down to talk, and he took me back to the day of his accident. He had become a Christian just a few months before that day. He had started a Bible study and was excited about this new adventure in his life. The future looked bright, and Michael was on top of the world.

One day when Michael was on patrol, a drunk driver tore past him. He called for backup and began to chase this out-of-control car. The impaired driver made it halfway through a curve when he hit an oncoming vehicle and knocked it out of its lane and into Michael's car. Michael tried to avoid hitting the car, but he couldn't. His car burst into flames.

The firemen arrived at Michael's blazing vehicle, and assuming he was dead, began to put out the inferno. When the rescue team saw that Michael was alive, they cut him out of his car and rushed him to the hospital. Michael had second-, third-, and fourth-degree burns on fifty percent of his body. His bullet-proof vest had protected his chest. But the doctors told his family that if he lived, they would have to amputate his left leg and both of his arms.

Michael lived. The amputations were performed. As Michael was slipping in and out of a drug induced stupor, he prayed, "God, you have spared me for a reason. I trust You to show me that reason."

As a result of the accident, Michael's face is distorted, and one of his ears is completely gone. He has no hair, and the skin around his eyes is badly scarred and melted—it looks as if it is painful just to open his eyes. Who would blame Michael if he wanted to hide away in a darkened room? Who would wonder if he questioned the love and care of this heavenly Father he had just discovered?

Suffering is seldom an item on our list of requests to

the Lord. But when it crosses our path and we are able by His grace to keep on walking, our lives become messages of hope to the world and to the church. There are plenty of examples from Scripture of people who suffered either from physical pain or loss or from spiritual persecution. Job suffered the loss of his property and his children. David suffered political and spiritual persecution. He was chased by Saul's men, captured by the Philistines, threatened by the followers of Baal. The apostle Peter lived in the New Testament era, during a period of intense religious persecution, and was eventually martyred upside down on a cross. In each case, we read of these men's commitment to God and their understanding that God's glory would be seen through their sufferings.

Job's response to his suffering was worship and trust in God:

"The LORD gave, and the LORD has taken away.
Blessed be the name of the LORD" (Job 1:21).

Job's trust in God was shaken for a time. Visited by friends who questioned him and his faith in God, Job finally joined in the questioning—quietly at first, then loudly and angrily. After days (perhaps months or years—no time is given in the book of Job) of this, God visited Job from a whirlwind.

"Where were you when I laid the foundations of the earth?" God asked. Who are you, a mere man, to condemn My judgment? How can you understand My wisdom, My reasons for doing things?

Job's final response was the same as his first: worship and trust.

"I know that You can do everything.
And that no purpose of Yours can be withheld from
    You. . . .
I have uttered what I did not understand,
Things too wonderful for me, which I did not know"
    (Job 12:2–3).

Job acknowledged that God was infinitely wise, and he, a mere man would never be able to comprehend all of God's purposes. Instead of questioning God further, Job would bow before Him and trust Him. When Job did this, God was honored in front of all of Job's friends.

David lived on the run. He was captured and held prisoner by the Philistines. He was threatened by Saul and pursued by Saul's army. He suffered the torment of the followers of Baal. Yet, amidst his torment, he turned to God:

> Vows made to You are binding upon me, O
>   God;
> I will render praises to You,
> For You have delivered my soul from death.
> Have You not delivered my feet from falling,
> That I may walk before God
> In the light of the living? (Ps. 56:12–13).

David's response to his suffering was similar to Michael's "God, You have spared me for a reason." David

was thankful God had saved him, but also recognized God's purpose for him as he went on living: to "walk before God." David believed his purpose in this life was to be faithful to God and to honor Him. And his faithfulness would cause others to honor God.

Peter wrote almost an entire letter to believers, encouraging them not to be surprised if they suffered or were persecuted for the name of Jesus Christ. "Rejoice to the extent that you partake of Christ's sufferings," Peter wrote, "that when His glory is revealed, you may also be glad with exceeding joy." Scholars speculate that his letter was written during the days of Nero, the cruelest of the Roman emperors. Yet, Peter was telling the believers to be glad for their sufferings. When Christ finally returned in His glory, they would feel joy as great as the sorrow they endured from the persecution and ridicule and physical abuse. "Therefore," Peter wrote, "let those who suffer according to the will of God commit their souls to Him in doing good, as to a faithful Creator" (1 Pet. 4:19). Michael now travels across America to schools and colleges, telling his story. He lifts his head high and tells young people everywhere that although his body is burned his faith in Christ is alive and well. Michael is overjoyed that Christ's glory is revealed as thousands see that his faith in God has withstood his scars and come through as refined as pure gold.

To the Unknown God

For as I was passing through and considering the objects of your worship, I even found an altar with this inscription:

TO THE UNKNOWN GOD.

Therefore, the One whom you worship without knowing, Him I proclaim to you.
Acts 17:23

I've been interested in the work of overseas missions since I was a child. My mother was a missionary secretary in our home church, so I heard a lot about the work that was going on in various parts of the world. At times, missionaries home on furlough would come to our house for dinner and I would sit and listen to their tales for hours. I decided that when I grew up I would be a missionary in India. I don't think I gave much thought to how I would serve these people. I guess I saw myself leading them in a few choruses of "Kum Ba Yah."

Once a month, in the winter time, the ladies in our church would gather in one of their homes and knit sweaters for African children. I remember thinking, *This*

is nuts. These poor little children are out there baking in the hot African sun and here we are knitting them sweaters.

As I grew older, I began to wonder *How do you communicate with a foreign culture and people? There has to be more than simply teaching them "Jesus Loves Me" in Swahili.*

Don Richardson understands more about this than anyone I have ever met. A missionary and linguist, Don directs tribal people studies at William Carey International University in Pasadena, California.

Don worked long and hard to communicate and establish a relationship with the Sawi people, a stone age tribe of tree dwellers, headhunters, and cannibals. He was finally able to sit down with the Sawis and tell them the Gospel story. However, when he got to the part about Judas Iscariot's betrayal of Jesus, the Sawis applauded.

The Sawi admired and modeled themselves after a group of warriors called the Masters of Treachery. This tribe would establish friendships with people with the intention of slaughtering them. Judas fit the mold of the Masters perfectly. He stayed by Christ's side, shared Christ's confidences, and then, at the right moment, betrayed Jesus.

Don could have given up when he saw how difficult communication with these people would be. But, believing God has prepared a way in the heart of every man, woman, and child of every creed and culture to receive and understand the Gospel, Don prayed for wisdom.

A few weeks later, Don heard of a sacred Sawi ritual, the ritual of the peace child. Two warring tribes could make peace if the son of one chief was given to the other. This guaranteed freedom from future treachery. Don sat down with the Sawi people and told them the story of the ultimate "peace child," the Son of God. The Sawis understood, repented of their sins, and began to follow Jesus Christ. Today, there is a healthy, literate Sawi tribe with a flourishing church.

God speaks to us in whatever language we can understand. He created us with a longing to know Him, and He is "not far from each one of us" (Acts 17:27)—that is, He will make it possible to know Himself.

God sent Paul to preach the Gospel to the people in Athens because Paul understood the Greek way of thinking. On the day of Pentecost, God sent the Holy Spirit to the apostles, and they preached the Gospel in the many different languages of the people who had gathered in Jerusalem. God has even used creation to visually speak to people of His character so they can know Him: "For since the creation of the world His invisible attributes are clearly seen, being understood by the things that are made, even His eternal power and Godhead, so that they are without excuse" (Rom. 1:20).

The Gospel that reached the tribe of the cannibals can reach a rebellious teen, a distant husband, a struggling alcoholic—someone just may have to preach it in a different language. God has written His law on all of our hearts. We simply have to find the right key to unlock the door and the right words to introduce the unknown God.

A New Allegiance

"He who loves father or mother more than Me is not worthy of Me. And he who loves son or daughter more than Me is not worthy of Me."
Matthew 10:37

I've always found Matthew 10:37 confusing. We are instructed elsewhere in Scripture to love and honor our parents so our lives will be long and fruitful. This passage makes it clear, however, where our ultimate allegiance must lie.

Those of us with Christian parents don't have the dilemma of changing our loyalty from our parents to God. My mother is a Christian woman and has always encouraged me to do whatever God tells me to do, no matter what. Don Smarto was not so blessed. Born into a family with roots in organized crime, Smarto was driven to God by fear.

Don's father was a gambler and a heavy drinker. He would often come home after his nights out, waving a large black revolver in the air and threatening the family.

In the midsixties, Don went to Kansas where he began

seminary and entered the priesthood. He was disillusioned by the many priests he met who seemed to care little for their faith, as if they were putting on a show of a "pious" life. Don wanted to find a real relationship with God.

One afternoon Don went to the movie theater to see an obscure movie about the Catholic church. The portrayal was irreverent and scathing. But one scene arrested Smarto's attention. The priest on the screen stood, the wind blowing around him. A sudden gust blew open his vestments, revealing a rotting skeleton underneath.

I'm that priest, Don thought. *I have a form of religion. But inside I'm a skeleton—I'm dead.*

Don left the theater and drove into the Kansas countryside. Parking his car, he walked across a cornfield and cried to the sky, "Who is that man on the Cross?" At that moment, the moon cast a shadow across a telephone pole, creating a giant cross.

Christ died for me! Don grabbed the pole and clung to the wood as he wept tears of joy. The Holy Spirit had revealed the truth to Don as he stood there.

Don Smarto's new adventure of faith was not an easy journey. He tried to share his joy with his family, but they were offended by his fervency. His brother, Anthony, tried to use his good priest brother as a cover, offering him $15,000. "Take it. You need some cash." Don refused the money, unsure of where his brother had "earned" it. But a few days later, two FBI agents came to Don's door, looking for Anthony.

The agents asked Don if Anthony had ever offered him money. Smarto longed to cover for his brother. The

family begged and threatened him. But Don couldn't stand before God and lie. He knew he was not worthy to be Christ's if his love for Christ was not greater than his love of his family. He acknowledged his brother's offer and was subpoenaed to testify at his brother's trial.

Before He died, Jesus warned the disciples that they would be persecuted because of their belief in Him. "I did not come to bring peace but a sword," Jesus said (Matt. 10:34). The abundant life would not be easy. Instead, He promised that His followers would be persecuted and hated for their belief and obedience. They would be brought before governors and kings. Even family members would deliver believers to be killed.

Don was placing his love for God before a family who easily could have destroyed him. Yet, he held fast to the hope of God's mercy and compassion. "He who endures to the end will be saved," Jesus said. "Do not fear those who kill the body but cannot kill the soul. But rather fear Him who is able to destroy both soul and body in hell. Are not two sparrows sold for a copper coin? And not one of them falls to the ground apart from your Father's will. But the very hairs of your head are all numbered. Do not fear therefore; you are of more value than many sparrows" (Matt. 10:22, 28–31). God knows every hair on our heads. He knows when harm comes to us, and He will save those who remained faithful despite suffering. If our love of our family is greater than our love of Jesus, we are not worthy to be His.

Don's testimony helped send his brother Anthony away for twenty years. Don is now an outcast from his family. He has committed the unpardonable sin of betrayal.

Don had to make a terrible choice, but he knows Christ did not come to bring peace. Although it has not been easy, he has found in Christ a better way to live.

The Sun Is Shining

"Do not fear, Daniel, for from the first day that you set your heart to understand, and to humble yourself before your God, your words were heard; and I have come because of your words."
Daniel 10:12

*C*athy Mahone was swept off her feet by Ali Bayon. A dark, handsome man from Jordan, Ali had come to college in America, where he met Cathy. Although he was a Moslem, religion was never an issue between them. Cathy had little interest in spiritual things, and Ali didn't practice his faith.

A year after Cathy and Ali were married, Cathy became a Christian. Ali was content to let her attend church and read the Bible, as long as she didn't expect him to accompany her. Cathy prayed God would one day change Ali's heart. She didn't expect the change that did take place.

When Cathy was five months pregnant, Ali visited his family in Jordan by himself. He returned a different man. Now fervently committed to Islam, Ali began to insist

154

their child be raised in the Moslem faith. Dumbfounded, Cathy did her best to keep peace in the household until Lauren was born. Then, she and Ali argued constantly. A year later, they divorced.

Cathy and Ali managed to establish a fairly amicable relationship, with Ali frequently seeing his daughter.

When Lauren was seven years old, Ali took her for the weekend, promising to drop her off at school on Monday morning. Monday afternoon, Cathy arrived at school to pick up Lauren. But she discovered Lauren had never been there.

Kidnapped! Cathy panicked. She knew instinctively what had happened. She ran inside the school and called the airport to confirm her suspicions. Ali and Lauren had, in fact, left for Jordan that morning.

Cathy immediately called the State Department, but they could offer little help. According to Jordanian law, the father has all legal rights to a child when the child is seven years old. So Ali had the right to take Lauren as his. The Department promised to try to help her but informed her that she was only one of many such cases.

Unable to bear going home to an empty house, Cathy checked into a cheap motel. She fasted and prayed for three days, begging God to speak to her. She opened her Bible and began to read in the book of Daniel: "Do not fear, Daniel, for from the first day that you set your heart to understand, and to humble yourself before your God, your words were heard; and I have come because of your words."

Daniel had prayed for help for twenty-one days and heard no answer. When the angel finally appeared to

him, he told him that God had heard Daniel the first day he prayed. "But the prince of the kingdom of Persia withstood me twenty-one days; and behold, Michael, one of the chief princes, came to help me, for I had been left alone there with the kings of Persia" (Dan. 10:13). The angel had immediately been sent to help Daniel but had been held back by a strong spiritual power of darkness. Because Daniel kept praying, the angel received more help and was able to come to Daniel.

Daniel's story gave Cathy hope to keep on praying. She knew she had done all she could do physically. Only God could bring Lauren back. Cathy left the hotel and went home, committing to pray each day and to wait.

Cathy didn't have to wait long for the first help to come. Only a few days later, one of a four-man covert commando team of ex-Delta force fighters heard of Cathy's plight and contacted her. He brought the team to meet with Cathy, and they planned to fly to Jordan and bring Lauren home. Three of the men were Christians and felt that God had sent them to fight on her behalf. The men told Cathy they would probably be executed if they were caught. But they were committed to the mission.

The men left for Jordan, promising to call Cathy when their rescue was complete. The code of victory was "The sun is shining."

For the next month, Cathy waited by the phone with no word. Finally, she decided to fly to Jordan to join the men.

The first day after Cathy joined the team, they spotted

Ali's car in a side street. The rescue mission was underway.

Phase One: The group would follow Lauren's school bus the next morning and hold it up in the countryside. Phase Two: Make a dash for Israel. They would be safe once they crossed the border.

Damp fog shrouded the city the next morning. Cathy's heart pounded as she and the men got in the car and followed Lauren's schoolbus, maintaining a careful distance from the bus. As soon as the bus left the city limits, the rescue team sped up, overtaking the bus and making it stop. Cathy lept from her car, raced onto the bus, and grabbed a startled Lauren.

Packed into the car, Cathy, Lauren, and the team headed toward the border. The fog slowed them, and Cathy wondered what would happen when they were pulled over at the checkpoint. She held Lauren tightly to her chest and looked out of the car window. A few miles away, she saw the Israeli border. And through a break in the clouds, the sun was shining. Cathy knew they were home free.

Today, Cathy and Lauren are together. Lauren prays every night that Jesus will touch her father's heart. Cathy has learned not to be discouraged by the apparent silence of heaven but, instead, to keep praying. Wars as real as those on earth are waged in the heavenly realm on behalf of those who love God.

Learning to Trust

When my father and my mother forsake me,
Then the LORD will take care of me.
Psalm 27:10

I toured Australia with Christian artist David Meece. He seemed quiet and a little difficult to get to know. But I discovered through time the horror of his childhood.

David's father was a respectable pharmacist. But behind the mask of professional success, he was an alcoholic and a rageaholic.

When David was eleven years old, his father came into his bedroom one evening with a gun. He pointed the gun at David's head and threatened to kill him and his brother. David's mother and grandmother managed to take the gun away from the father. Soon after that episode, David's parents divorced.

David felt he had caused his parents' problems. He began to think, *If I were a better kid, my Dad wouldn't drink and my Mom wouldn't get beat up.* David never discussed the pain or the problems with his family. He denied his grief, instead, and replaced it with the drive to succeed.

158

David became a Christian at college but kept a tight lid on his past. When his father died, he stood over the casket and felt nothing. Inside, however, the quiet storm was intensifying.

A year later he sought a doctor because he thought he was having a heart attack. The doctor diagnosed him as having had an anxiety attack. Intuitively, he asked David if anyone in his family had a problem with alcohol. David acknowledged that his father had had a drinking problem, but he refused the doctor's advice to get help for himself.

A year passed after David had seen the doctor about his anxiety attack. One evening after a concert, David returned to his motel room where he broke down, weeping. There, God gave David a vision of his father as a little boy, trembling and alone, full of fear. David had compassion on his father and forgave him that night, making peace with his past.

David Meece began to trust as the David of the Bible did: "When my mother and father forsake me, / Then the LORD will take care of me." This verse may seem confusing because King David's parents never left him. He had been persecuted, however. Wicked men had chased him. False witnesses had testified against him. But David was not afraid. "The LORD is my light and my salvation," the psalmist wrote. "Whom shall I fear? / The LORD is the strength of my life." David knew his protector. Armies could surround him; war could rise against him; even his parents could leave him. He would expect God to be his strength amidst adversity (Ps. 27:1).

Confident of God's love and protection, David Meece

was able to share this love with his father through forgiveness. He was no longer a slave to the addiction of his earthly father. Instead, he found the love of his heavenly father and was freed of anger and bitterness and anxiety. He proclaimed with the psalmist:

> I would have lost heart, unless I had believed
> That I would see the goodness of the LORD
> In the land of the living (Ps. 27:13).

Meece learned to follow God without faltering or becoming discouraged and giving up.

We would all like to be loved and cared for by two parents who have our best interests at heart, though that seems to be a luxury these days. But we do have a forever promise: God has committed Himself to fill the gap. If your father or mother has abandoned you, the Lord will take care of you. Learning to trust again was difficult for David Meece. It began with one baby step, led by a committed Father.

When God Won't Bail You Out

> If we say that we have fellowship with Him, and
> walk in darkness, we lie and do not practice the
> truth.
> 1 John 1:6

*D*ishonesty begins in little ways. We leave work
early or take a few supplies home with us. We're tired or
bored, so we call in sick. As believers, we often think if
we do get in trouble, God will bail us out. But that's not
always so.

Stan Peerless was a successful attorney who special-
ized in real estate. He and his wife decided to put themselves on a strict budget and build their own home. As
the house went up, so did the costs. Luxuries and extras
were liberally thrown in, and soon Stan was in a house-
shaped hole with no escape hatch.

Desperate to dig himself out of this mess, Stan turned
to what seemed to be the only solution. As a real estate
lawyer, he held a bank account with clients' money that
was to be used for closing costs. He would write himself
checks from that account.

A Bible-believing, churchgoing man, Stan reasoned away his intentions. The money was just sitting there. The amount in the account constantly fluctuated, so it would be hard for anyone to tell if it was correct or not. He wasn't going to steal. He fully intended to repay every cent he borrowed. He simply needed to buy himself some time.

Stan started with fifty or a hundred dollars. Then, he increased the amount to a thousand; then four thousand. Before he could stop himself, he had accumulated a debt of more than $350,000.

In numbed disbelief, Peerless turned himself in. He was convicted on four counts of embezzlement and sentenced to ten years in prison.

Stan must have felt devastated—a Christian man with the best of intentions, sitting in prison alone, day after day. He had lost his integrity, his wholeness. Removed from his world and responsibilities, Stan realized that his life had become fragmented. He had to start over, being consistent in his thinking and beliefs and his decisions.

Peerless began to pray and study and reflect on his life. When he was released from prison, he and his wife, Linda, began seeing a marriage counselor. They lost their savings and their home. But they found themselves and the strength to begin to walk with integrity before the Lord.

I wonder how many well-intentioned people are one day away from the biggest mistake of their lives? The Old Testament King David stayed home from war one day and fell into an affair with a woman named Bathsheba that led to the conception of a child and, later, the arranged murder of the woman's husband. When he was finally confronted with his sin, David, too, had to recover the pieces of his fragmented life. He had to start over just as Stan had to start over.

"Behold, You desire truth in the inward parts," David prayed after his conviction. He had tried to hide his sin. But when God sent the prophet Nathan to reveal his sin, he realized God had known the truth all along. David quit running and took time alone to pray and be restored to God. His prayer is recorded in Psalm 51:

> Have mercy upon me, O God,
> According to Your lovingkindness;
> According to the multitude of Your tender mercies,
> Blot out my transgressions.
> Wash me thoroughly from my iniquity.
> And cleanse me from my sin.
> For I acknowledge my transgressions,
> And my sin is ever before me.
> Against You, You only, have I sinned,
> And done this evil in Your sight.

David realized that it was God he had sinned against, so he didn't expect God to bail him out or help him cover up. He acknowledged his sin and asked for God's cleansing. He expected God to be merciful. He believed God's kindness was not limited, that he had a "multitude" of "tender mercies" and His Spirit was "generous." And God proved David true as seen in the conclusion of the story in 2 Samuel 12.

David took Bathsheba as his wife and conceived an-

other son with her. "So she bore a son, and he called his name Solomon. And the LORD loved him." God showed His mercy was unlimited by restoring David and loving David and his son.

We can maintain an appearance of integrity, fudging here and there, promising ourselves we'll make up for our actions somehow. We can hope God will make up for our sin. But we can only share in God's life by living honestly. God desires "truth in the inward part"—He wants us to live as honestly when people aren't watching as we do when they are.

Each time we turn away from the gentle whispers of the Holy Spirit pointing out our discrepancies, we become increasingly deaf. We can end up far away from God without realizing we've moved.

Somebody's Praying for Me

Praying always with all prayer and supplication
in the Spirit, being watchful to this end with all
perseverance and supplication for all the saints.
Ephesians 6:18

I sat at my desk one afternoon in December 1991, my
head in my hands, my heart heavy. The year that lay
ahead would be one of the most critical years of my life.
Questions to which I could find no answers raced
through my mind. Choices loomed before me.

Evening fell as I grappled with my future. I was tired
and alone, and I felt as if I were being torn apart.

Suddenly, the heaviness lifted from me. I didn't understand at first. I had no answers. I had made no decisions. Then, I knew. Someone was praying for me.

It was one of the most incredible moments of my life. I
didn't know who was praying or what he knew about
my struggle. But I knew that someone was down on his
knees on my behalf.

I went out into the chill night air and sat at the end of
our boat dock, under the stars—at peace and not alone.

Paul told the Ephesians to pray always, "being watchful to this end." The end he referred to was "to quench all the fiery darts of the wicked one" (Eph. 6:16). He warned believers to hold on to their faith in God so they would be protected against Satan's attack—the discouragement and guilt and despair he can use successfully to keep us from continuing to walk with the Lord. As we take up the "shield of faith," we can pray for our brothers and sisters, that we will all be able to persevere, to stand to the end, until the Lord returns.

People often tell me they pray for me. But until that December night, I didn't realize how much I needed their prayers. When these difficult days are behind me and, by God's grace, I am still standing, one of the reasons will be that someone prayed for me.

Somebody's Praying for Me

Somebody's praying for me tonight
I can feel my heart starting to mend
I don't know who you are
But deep down in my heart
I know somebody's praying for me.

Somebody's praying for me tonight
Do you think they can tell I'm alone?
Through a careful disguise
Behind smiling brown eyes
Somebody's praying for me.

Some days I feel I could conquer the world,
Some days I feel like a fool
And when I feel very small
When I've no strength at all
That's when somebody's praying for me.

Thank you Father for the ones
Who pray upon the walls
Their faces hidden from the crowds
But known in heaven's halls.

Somebody's praying for me
Somebody's praying for me
I know that out in the crowd there is
Someone who's praying for me.
Somebody's praying for me
Here in my heart I believe
Somebody's praying for me
I can feel, someone's praying for me.

167

Made Ready by Suffering

I have suffered the loss of all things, and count
them as rubbish, . . . that I may know Him and
the power of His resurrection, and the fellowship
of His sufferings, being conformed to His death.
Philippians 3:8, 10

*K*athy and Steve Bartalsky felt called to the mission
field. Steve was a helicopter pilot and had been accepted
to work in Camaroon with Helimission, a group that
reaches otherwise inaccessible areas and tribes with the
Gospel and medical supplies. Steve and Kathy had a
brand new baby girl, and friends and family warned
them to wait until she was older to go overseas. But the
Bartalskys believed their little one would be fine.

Just before they left, Steve and Kathy's baby was diagnosed with spinal meningitis. She died when she was
three months old.

The Bartalskys postponed their trip while they
grieved their loss. As they were recovering, their desire
to serve grew stronger than ever. At last they adopted a
boy, Colby, and the three of them left for Camaroon.

Helimission has a unique and focused vision. Poisonous gas killed 1700 people at Lake Nyof during 1986, and the Helimission team was able to fly out the survivors. After the village people had reestablished themselves in the area, the Helimission pilots flew in sixty-five Bible students and 1346 people gave their lives to Christ.

Steve and Kathy knew they were right in the center of God's will for their lives by participating in the mission. Despite tough times, they had an unmistakable peace that comes from being where you should be.

Steve flew supplies into Uganda one day. To get there, he left from the capital of Camaroon, which was six hours from the village where Steve and Kathy lived. Steve and Kathy decided Kathy would leave Colby with a friend and then drive to the capital to pick up Steve when he returned.

Kathy did as planned and was there to hug Steve as he stepped onto the tarmac. The couple went inside for a cold drink before the long drive home. Just before they left, they received a telephone call.

Colby had accidently drunk some poison. He was dead.

Kathy and Steve drove home in shocked silence.

A day later, Kathy and Steve buried their second child—this time in a foreign grave.

Kathy questioned God in agony. "Why would You do this to us a second time? We are here because You called us. Where is the sense in all this suffering?" She thought of the verse in Psalms that promised that those who honored God would live to see their children around their

table. *What could it mean?* she wondered, for here she and Steve sat alone, two children dead before they were.

Kathy's sufferings drove her to look long and hard into the face of God to see if He was still a loving God. As she looked and questioned, God showed her a new level of love and gave her a new passion to serve Him, no matter what the cost.

Two months later Steve and Kathy moved to Addis Ababa in Ethiopia to fly famine relief. They forgot their own pain as they strove to help meet the needs and relieve the devastation of the people in the area. But tragedy soon visited the couple again.

Only three months after Steve and Kathy had settled in Addis Ababa, a group of men came to Kathy's door. One stepped forward.

"Kathy—it's Steve." All of the men looked solemn as the spokesman continued. "His helicopter crashed today when he went out, Kathy. There wasn't anything we could have done. He's—Steve's dead."

"Every time I thought I had given it all to Him," Kathy told me in an interview as she recounted the events, "I found there was more to give."

Her words reminded me of Paul's letter to the Philippians: "But indeed I also count all things loss for the excellence of the knowledge of Christ Jesus my Lord, for whom I have suffered the loss of all things, and count them as rubbish, that I may gain Christ and be found in Him, . . . that I may know Him and the power of His resurrection, and the fellowship of His sufferings, being conformed to His death, if, by any means, I may attain to the resurrection from the dead" (Phil. 3:8–11). Paul lost

everything; yet, he felt his losses were rubbish—literally, from the Greek, *dung*—compared with the gain of Christ Jesus.

Paul longed more to know Christ and to be a partner with Christ in His pain than he did to hang on to his status or his righteousness that came from keeping the law. Kathy's longing to know Christ was greater than her desire to hang on to her two children and husband or to have them somehow brought back. She allowed herself to become a partner in Christ's sufferings through her grief. And she pressed on as Paul did: "forgetting those things which are behind and reaching forward to those things which are ahead, I press toward the goal for the prize of the upward call of God in Christ Jesus" (Phil. 3:13–14).

Kathy had Steve's friends take her to the sight where his helicopter had crashed. There, at the clearing in the woods where her husband's mangled machinery lay, Kathy felt as if she were on holy ground. Steve had gone home to victory in that clearing. Kathy wanted to take off her shoes.

"If we believe in God only for the blessing He can give us," Kathy told me, "our belief in Him is not based on love and trust but on our own selfish desires and our own concept of what we think God owes us."

Kathy is happy. She is still young and attractive; she has not been hardened by her pain. But when I look at Kathy, I feel as if the frivolity of life has been stripped away from her. She has left behind many of the things that don't matter and is clinging to the best God has to give—Himself.

Knowing Kathy has helped me believe for the first time that you can be glad when you suffer because it makes you ready for what really matters and what will last forever.

Epilogue

I want to leave a brighter trail
for those who come behind
I want to be a candle burning
in the darkest night
I want to be a shoulder strong
enough for crying on
I want to carry those whose
shoes are worn
I want to tell the smallest child
Look up, you're not alone
I want to take the oldest face
and hold it to my own
I want to sing from every hill
and shout from every wall
Because He lives
there's mercy for us all.